Maryland

Maryland

Michael Burgan

Children's Press®
A Division of Grolier Publishing
New York   London   Hong Kong   Sydney
Danbury, Connecticut

Frontispiece: Chesapeake Bay

Front cover: Sailboat on Chesapeake Bay

Back cover: Baltimore row houses

Consultant: Suzanne Guardia, Assistant Director of Education, Maryland Historical Society, Baltimore

Please note: All statistics are as up-to-date as possible at the time of publication.

Visit Children's Press on the Internet at http://publishing.grolier.com

Book production by Editorial Directions, Inc.

Library of Congress Cataloging-in-Publication Data

Burgan, Michael.
   Maryland / Michael Burgan.
     144 p. 24 cm. — (America the beautiful. Second series)
   Includes bibliographical references and index.
   Summary : Describes the geography, plants and animals, history, economy, language, religions, culture, and people of Maryland.
   ISBN 0-516-21039-4
   1. Maryland—Juvenile literature. [1. Maryland.] I. Title. II. Series.
  F181.3.B87   1999
  975.2—dc21
                                                 98-42164
                                                   CIP
                                                      AC

GROLIER
PUBLISHING

Acknowledgments

I would like to thank Anne Mannix at the Maryland Office of Tourism Development; Nancy Hinds at the Baltimore Area Convention and Visitors Association; and all the other Marylanders who showed me great courtesy and gave me valuable information while I wrote this book. Special thanks to Matt Brenneman for his hospitality.

Fishing in Maryland

The Potomac river

On the Appalachian Trail

Cal Ripken Jr.

Contents

Tobacco

Annapolis

The USS *Constellation*

Thoroughbred horses

CHAPTER ONE

America in Miniature

The western shore of Chesapeake Bay

Along the waters of Maryland's Chesapeake Bay, fishers on sailing ships haul in their daily catch, just as they did hundreds of years ago. The bay has provided food and jobs for Marylanders since colonial days, playing a key role in the state's history. And long before Europeans saw those waters, Native Americans also turned to the bay for their daily needs.

The Chesapeake Bay is known as an *estuary*—a place where saltwater and freshwater meet. The salt comes from the nearby Atlantic Ocean, while more than twenty freshwater rivers pour into the bay. The Chesapeake's waters hold oysters, crabs, and a variety of fish. Waterfowl, such as ducks, geese, and osprey, live along its marshes. Almost cutting Maryland in two, the bay's shoreline in the state is 3,190 miles (5,134 km) long. With such easy access to water, early Marylanders became pioneers in shipbuilding and the transporting of goods.

The Chesapeake helps define the geography and economy of Maryland—and its spirit as well. But the state is more than oysters and egrets along a shoreline dotted with quaint sailing boats. In the 1920s, a visiting writer said Maryland, with its variety of land and resources, was "America in miniature." The Chesapeake region is a flat, coastal plain, but in the western edge of the state, the Appalachian Mountains rise up more than 3,000 feet (900 m).

Opposite: A royal tern colony at Chesapeake Bay

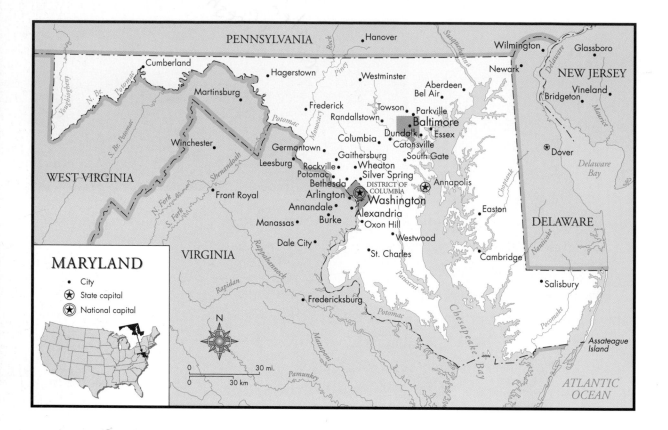

Geopolitical map of Maryland

Between the bay and the mountains, rolling hills feature farms that grow corn, soybeans, tobacco, and plants and trees for homes.

Fishing and farming are ties to Maryland's past, but the state also has deep roots as a birthplace for industry and inventions. In the nineteenth century, the United States's first regular railroad service began in Maryland. The state has also been the site of major developments in air transportation. Today, high-tech industries lead the way in conducting medical research and developing computer software.

Maryland is also home to many government offices. In 1791,

Maryland donated the land that became Washington, D.C., and the country's lawmakers have since returned the favor by making Maryland an important place for government facilities. From the testing of new weapons at the Aberdeen Proving Ground to the testing of new medicines at the Food and Drug Administration, Americans rely on the service of Marylanders working for their government.

The Mix of Maryland

The Marylanders who fish the state's waters and pore over test tubes in its labs are a diverse group of people. Just as the Chesapeake Bay blends waters from the ocean and rivers, Maryland blends people from many different backgrounds. The first European settlers were English, but they were soon followed by Germans, Irish, Italians, Jews, and a host of other immigrants. The city of Baltimore, Maryland's largest, was a major port of arrival for these newcomers and for other immigrants who fanned out across America.

Soon after the first Europeans came, Africans were brought to Maryland, usually as slaves. With its slavery and plantation farming, Maryland was more like a southern state than a northern one. Yet its industry and its thriving port of Baltimore made it similar to

Fishing has always been an important part of Maryland life.

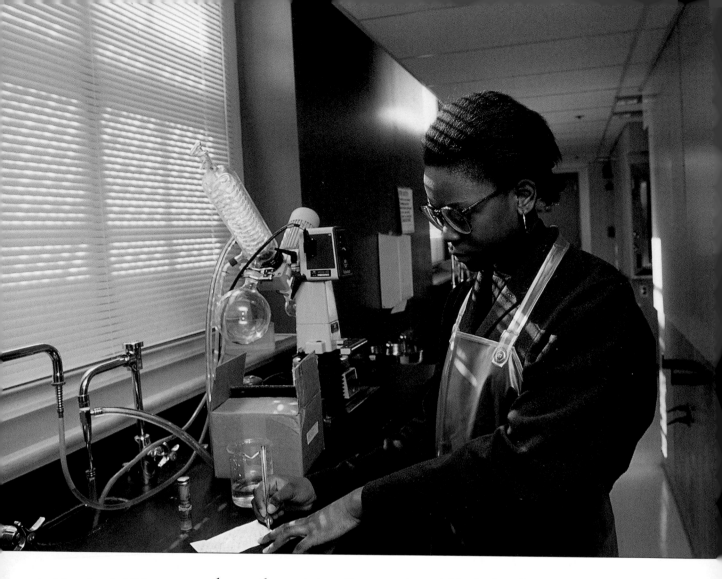

In Maryland, African-Americans make up 25 percent of the population.

the northern states. Once again, within its borders Maryland was almost a mirror of the country as a whole.

Maryland also had more free blacks than most southern states, and some won national fame. Free blacks developed their own community in Baltimore, and though they did not escape racism, they found better lives than many blacks who lived farther south. Today, African-Americans make up 25 percent of Maryland's population.

Historically, Maryland also had a great mix of religious faiths, which still exists today. Founded by Roman Catholics from England, Maryland developed a reputation for tolerating people of many faiths—Protestants, Jews, and more recent arrivals of other religious backgrounds.

Maryland in the Middle

In 1634, one of the first Europeans to settle in Maryland was Father Andrew White, a Catholic priest from England. He compared Maryland to New England to the north and Virginia to the south. His new home, he wrote, had "a middle temperature between the two, and enjoys the advantages, and escapes the evils, of each." Almost 300 years later, Baltimore writer H. L. Mencken offered a similar view of his state. Compared to other states, in population and climate, Maryland had a "safe middle place." It had a balance of city dwellers (mostly in Baltimore) and rural people. Maryland, Mencken wrote, was "the ideal toward which the rest of the Republic is striving."

Today, Maryland is still a balance, a mixture of land, people, and ideas. Although small in size, it has made important contributions to America's politics, commerce, and art. In many ways, Maryland *is* America in miniature.

CHAPTER TWO

Land of Freedom

Smoke curled from small fires, and groups of women tended corn in the fields. Along Chesapeake Bay, men searched for fish or hunted game. People lived peacefully in small villages scattered on either side of the bay.

This scene was typical for the first residents of Maryland. They belonged to various Algonquin tribes, a Native American people who lived along the northern coast of the Atlantic Ocean. Indians first came to Maryland about 10,000 B.C. Over the centuries, they discovered the plentiful oysters in the bay, farmed the land, and created a thriving society.

Giovanni da Verrazano was the first European to see the waters of the Chesapeake Bay.

The First Europeans

In 1524, the Italian explorer Giovanni da Verrazano sailed past Chesapeake Bay and became the first European to see its waters. John Smith, one of the founders of the nearby Jamestown colony in Virginia, mapped the bay in 1608. About two decades later, William Claiborne set up a post on Kent Island in the bay to trade with the local Indians.

Unlike these earlier visitors, the group led by Leonard Calvert came to North America to develop a permanent colony. Calvert's father, George, had won the right to settle Maryland from England's King Charles I. George Calvert, a close adviser of King James I

Opposite: The Bay of Annapolis in the 1880s

The Indians of Maryland

When Europeans first landed in Maryland, many Indian villages dotted both sides of Chesapeake Bay. On the Eastern Shore lived the Choptank, Nanticoke, Pocomoke, and Assateague tribes. On the west side, the tribes included the Yaocomaco, Piscataway, Potapaco, and Mattowoman. In all, about 3,000 native Americans lived in the region.

The Indian tribes had good relations with one another, and with the English settlers. When he landed in Maryland in 1634, Father Andrew White wrote, "The natives of person be very proper and tall men," and he described the Indians as civil and intelligent. The English were particularly friendly with the Yaocomaco, who gave the newcomers food, including roasted oysters from the bay. To improve their ties, the English offered the Indians protection from their common enemy, the Susquehannock. The Susquehannock had already wiped out many Algonquin-speaking people along the bay. This fierce tribe lived farther north, along a river that the colonists named after them. ■

and active in the English government, converted to Roman Catholicism in 1625 and left government service. That same year, he was awarded the title Lord Baltimore from King James. He then turned all his attention to starting a colony in North America.

In 1629, Lord Baltimore asked the new English king, Charles I, for land along the northern part of Chesapeake Bay, in what was then Virginia. The Protestant rulers there tried to prevent this Catholic lord from becoming their neighbor, but Calvert won royal approval for his plan. Unfortunately, the official word came two

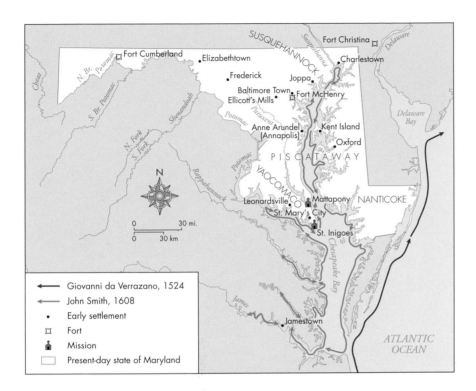

months after Calvert's death in April 1632. It was up to Calvert's sons, Cecilius and Leonard, to lead the settlement of Maryland.

Cecilius inherited the title Lord Baltimore from his father. He named the colony *Maryland* in honor of Henrietta Maria, wife of King Charles I, and appointed Leonard the leader of the Maryland expedition. As Catholics, the Calverts faced legal restrictions in England, where the Protestant Church of England was now the official religion. The Calverts wanted to practice their religion in Maryland without any government interference, but Cecilius also wanted "to preserve unity and peace" with the Protestants traveling with Leonard and in neighboring Virginia. Maryland was to be a land of religious tolerance.

Glimpse of the Past

St. Mary's City is located at the southern tip of the Chesapeake Bay's Western Shore, north of the Potomac River. Here, Leonard Calvert's group built a fort, then slowly added houses and other buildings, including a mint and a statehouse. After Maryland's capital moved to Annapolis in 1694, St. Mary's City lost its importance, but today this historic site is preserved as a "living museum."

Set on about 800 acres (320 ha), historic St. Mary's City recreates life in seventeenth-century Maryland. Throughout the town, actors in colonial dress explain the history of St. Mary's and the people who founded it. The town features original buildings from the past as well as replicas of an old tobacco farm and the first state house. On the water behind the state house sits the wooden sailing ship *Maryland Dove*, a replica of one of the ships that brought the first English settlers to the area.

St. Mary's City also has a model of a small Indian village, including a longhouse similar to the one used by the Yaocomaco and other American Indians. A monument dedicated to Leonard Calvert marks the spot where he and the Indians signed their first treaty. ■

From Indentured Servant to Public Servant

One of the passengers on the *Ark* was Mathias de Sousa. Half Portuguese and half African, he was the first black resident of Maryland. De Sousa arrived as an indentured servant—he received passage to America in exchange for his labor. Many poor Europeans, black and white, came to America this way. After working for up to seven years for their masters, the servants received their freedom.

De Sousa finished his term as an indentured servant in 1638 and became a sailor and fur trader. He also served as an interpreter between the English and the Native Americans. In 1641, he led a trading expedition to the Susquehannock Indians. The following year he was elected to the Maryland Colonial Assembly. Today, a plaque in St. Mary's City honors de Sousa's achievements. ■

Sailing on the *Ark* and the *Maryland Dove*, the settlers reached the Chesapeake Bay in March 1634. On March 25, they came ashore, and two days later Leonard Calvert bought land from the Yaocomaco Indians. He founded the first capital of Maryland, St. Mary's City, named for the mother of Jesus.

Early Government—and Conflicts

The colonists started their own government in St. Mary's City, with an elected General Assembly and Leonard Calvert as governor. In 1649, the Assembly made Calvert's desire for religious freedom official policy, passing the Religious Toleration Act—the first law of its kind in America. The Calvert family, however, did not remain in complete control of Maryland. Political and religious conflicts in England spilled over to the colony, and, during the 1650s, Puritan settlers challenged the Calverts' rule. With the

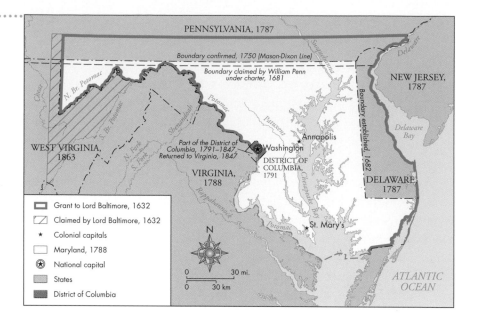

Puritans in control, Maryland's Catholics eventually lost their legal right to practice their faith in public. The Calvert rule was restored in 1657, but lost again in 1689 when the English Crown took over the colony.

Asking for "Vote and Voice"

In the seventeenth century, when men dominated society, Margaret Brent was an exception. Arriving in Maryland in 1638, Brent owned land and was active in business. Her skills impressed Governor Leonard Calvert. In 1647, as he was dying, Calvert asked Brent to take care of his estate after his death. She acted as his attorney, making her, in effect, America's first female lawyer.

In 1648, while representing Calvert's interests, Brent went to the General Assembly. According to the official record, she ". . . requested to have vote in the House for herself and voice also . . . as His Lordship's attorney." Her request was denied, despite her protests. Still, Brent had made the first recorded effort by an American woman to vote in a political assembly. ■

In 1692, the new English rulers made the Church of England Maryland's official church and three years they later moved the capital to Annapolis. The Calverts regained control once again in 1715. Although non-family members sometimes served as governor, the Calverts controlled Maryland until the American Revolution (1775–1783). Despite the years of political turmoil, Maryland attracted settlers of many faiths who, for the most part, lived together without conflict.

Slavery Comes to Maryland

The Maryland colonists found many ways to make a living. Some were merchants who sold goods to local residents. Other Marylanders turned to trade, taking advantage of easy access to rivers,

Slaves were sold to plantation owners at markets or auctions.

the bay, and the nearby Atlantic Ocean. Farmers grew a variety of crops, mostly for their own use. But one crop was sold in many lands and made fortunes for the families who grew it—tobacco.

Southern Maryland developed tobacco plantations, just as Virginia had. These plantations required many workers, so the farmers imported Africans to raise this important crop. In 1664, slavery became legal in the colony, and fewer Africans arrived as indentured servants, or people working for a specified period of time in return for travel expenses and maintenance. Over time, Maryland passed laws denying legal rights to free blacks and imported more slaves from Africa.

In the northern and western parts of the colony, however, the economy relied less on slaves. There, farmers owned smaller plots of land and did not need slave labor—or couldn't afford it. Later, in the eighteenth century, Germans began settling in western Maryland. Many of them belonged to religious groups that opposed slavery. Marylanders would continue to have contrasting attitudes about slavery through the American Civil War (1861–1865), and racism lasted well beyond that bloody struggle.

Birth of a Boomtown

In 1729, a small town named for Lord Baltimore was founded on the Patapsco River. The town was located near corn and tobacco farms and a road that led north to Philadelphia and south to Annapolis. Baltimore also had waterfalls to power mills, and easy access to the Chesapeake Bay. Taken together, these conditions helped turn Baltimore into an important center for trade and manufacturing.

Baltimore Town, as it was called, grew slowly. New land was bought, expanding its boundaries, and immigrants came to the city from other parts of North America and Europe. By the 1760s, the milling and shipping of wheat and flour became big business; so did shipbuilding and ocean trade. Baltimore's ships sailed to other American colonies, the Caribbean, and Europe. Annapolis was the capital of Maryland, but Baltimore was its commercial heart.

Baltimore became an important city known for trade and manufacturing.

Maryland Fights for Freedom

After winning the French and Indian War (1754–1763), Britain tried to tighten its rule over the American colonies. New taxes and legal restrictions upset many colonists, including Marylanders. In 1774, at the First Continental Congress (a gathering of delegates from all the colonies), the American representatives decided the colonies would protest this increasing loss of freedom by refusing to import goods from Britain.

In October of that year, Anthony Stewart, an Annapolis merchant, ignored the Congress's decision and accepted a shipment of tea from Britain. When Stewart's neighbors found out, they told him to burn the *Peggy Stewart*, the ship carrying the tea "or be hanged right there at your front door." Stewart chose to burn the ship. Like the famous Boston Tea Party of 1773, the *Peggy Stewart* incident showed the rising tensions in the colonies over British rule.

When the American Revolution began, in 1775, Marylanders played an important role. Baltimore privateers led the attacks on English shipping. These privately owned American ships had government permission to seize cargo from enemy ships. The privateers captured hundreds of ships during the first two years of the war. The state's troops also won praise for their skills during the war. "Nothing could exceed the gallantry of the Maryland Line," wrote American general Nathanael Greene. The Maryland "Old Line" fought with George Washington in the north and was soon famous for its bravery. Today, one of Maryland's nicknames is the "Old Line State."

The First National Government

As the fighting between American and British troops raged in the field, American politicians created the new country's first government. In March 1781, the Continental Congress approved the Articles of Confederation, which described the relationship between the Thirteen Colonies and the national government. John Hanson of Frederick, Maryland, was elected president of the new government.

The Articles of Confederation created a weak central government, and once the Revolutionary War for independence was won, some Americans began to call for a new system. At a convention

The Road to Statehood

On June 28, 1776, Maryland's political leaders decided to support the battle for American independence. Less than a week later, Maryland's four delegates to the Continental Congress— William Paca, Charles Carroll, Samuel Chase, and Thomas Stone—signed the Declaration of Independence (above).

In 1781, Maryland gave its approval to the Articles of Confederation. Daniel Carroll was Maryland's first representative to sign the document. On April 28, 1788, the state became the seventh to approve the Constitution. When the Constitution officially took effect in June 1788, thousands of people flooded into the streets of Baltimore to celebrate the birth of the new government. Later that year, Maryland government officials offered to donate land on the Potomac River for the site of a new national capital. The official transfer of this land, the District of Columbia, came in 1791. ■

held in Annapolis in 1786, the country's leaders made plans to meet in Philadelphia the following year to create that new government. The result was the U.S. Constitution, which introduced the national government we have today.

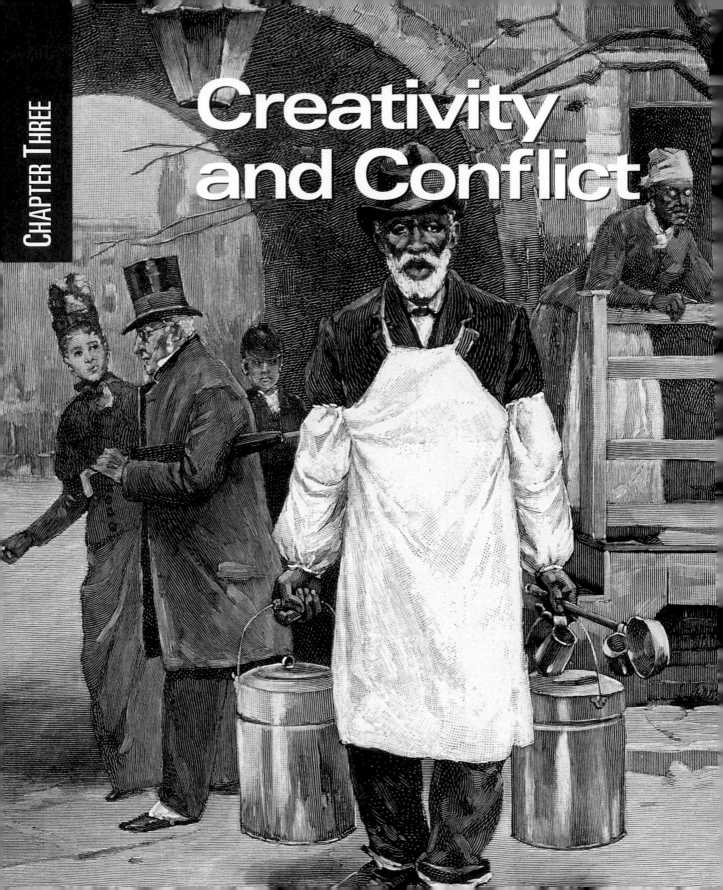

CHAPTER THREE

Creativity and Conflict

aryland in the early nineteenth century continued to grow. In Baltimore, inventors improved the methods for milling flour, making hats, and manufacturing metal goods. Merchants started new businesses, creating banks and some of America's first insurance companies. In the western part of Maryland, better roads improved travel between Baltimore and emerging new towns. Tobacco farmers in the south also prospered. But more trouble was brewing with Britain, and Maryland found itself in the middle of it.

Opposite: African-American oyster shucker

A Respected Scientist and Author

One of Maryland's first scientists was Benjamin Banneker. A self-taught mathematician and astronomer, Banneker was a free black who helped illustrate the intellectual equality of African-Americans at a time when racist thinking led many white people to doubt their talents.

Born in 1731 in Baltimore County, Banneker showed his skills as a young man when he built a wooden clock using a borrowed pocket watch as a model. He also recorded his observations of the modern world. Later, borrowing books and instruments from a neighbor, he taught himself astronomy. In 1791, Banneker was chosen to help survey the Maryland territory that became Washington, D.C.

The same year, Banneker won his greatest fame when he published an almanac. Like other almanacs of the era, Banneker's book had charts showing the phases of the moon and other astronomical information. But his book also had strong statements against slavery. Banneker sent a copy of the almanac to Thomas Jefferson, who said the work proved "nature has given our black brethren talents equal to those of the other colours of men." Banneker continued his scientific explorations and writing until his death in 1806. ■

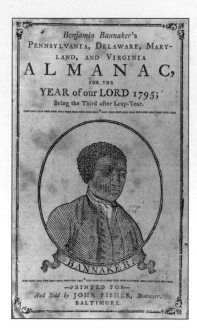

Benjamin Bannaker's
PENNSYLVANIA, DELAWARE, MARYLAND, AND VIRGINIA
ALMANAC,
FOR THE
YEAR of our LORD 1795;
Being the Third after Leap-Year.

BANNAKER

—PRINTED FOR—
And Sold by JOHN FISHER, Stationer,
BALTIMORE.

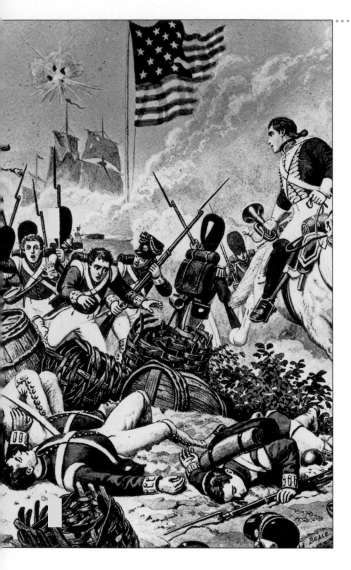

Baltimore played a vital role in the War of 1812.

The War of 1812

Problems with Britain began as early as 1805. British ships sailed off the Chesapeake Bay, stopping ships coming out of Maryland and Virginia. The British were searching for deserters from their navy, but many of the men they took were actually U.S. sailors. Tensions between the two countries grew, and in 1812 the United States declared war.

America and England fought a series of battles on land and at sea. In 1813, the British invaded Maryland and destroyed the town of Havre de Grace. The next year, President James Madison watched helplessly as the British marched into Washington, D.C., and burned it. Their next target was Baltimore, which the British considered "a nest of pirates." The city's defenders, however, were ready for battle.

The British began a land invasion on September 12, 1814, then held back for the second phase of the attack—a naval shelling of Fort McHenry. But the U.S. troops at this fort on the edge of Baltimore Harbor withstood the constant bombardment and fought off another land attack. The British withdrew, and the heroic defense of Baltimore inspired Francis Scott Key, a lawyer and poet, to write "The Star-Spangled Banner."

Stars and Stripes over Baltimore

From the deck of a ship not far from Fort McHenry, Francis Scott Key watched the attack on Baltimore. Key, a native of Frederick, Maryland, had boarded the ship in an effort to win the freedom of a friend who had been arrested by the British.

The British assault on the fort lasted for about twenty-five hours, featuring cannonballs and a new weapon, the Congreve rocket. The rockets streaked across the night sky before exploding, but they were not accurate and caused little damage to the fort. Only two Americans were killed during the long bombardment.

On the morning of September 14, 1814, as the fort's band played "Yankee Doodle," the victorious American troops at Fort McHenry raised a U.S. flag, 30 by 42 feet (9 by 13 m). The fort's commander, Major George Armistead, had asked Baltimore seamstress Mary Pickersgill to sew the huge flag so that the British would be sure to see it. After witnessing the battle and the stirring sight of the flying flag, Key wrote, "My heart spoke, and 'Does not such a country and such defenders of their country deserve a song?' was its question."

Key then wrote these lines: "Oh say can you see, by the dawn's early light . . . " Key called his finished poem "Defence of Fort McHenry," but it's now known as "The Star-Spangled Banner," the words to America's national anthem. ■

The "Iron Horse"

In the years after the War of 1812, peace brought greater prosperity to America. The nation's first national highway, the National Road, opened in 1818, linking Cumberland, in the northwest corner of Maryland, to Wheeling, Virginia (now in West Virginia). Maryland, like the rest of the country was also hit with "canal fever." States hoped to improve transportation and lower shipping costs by digging canals to link rivers with one another or with large lakes. Maryland began work on the Chesapeake and Ohio Canal in 1828, to link the Potomac and Ohio Rivers. But even more exciting—and more important for the future of the state—was the coming of the railroad.

After visiting Britain, Marylander Evan Howard returned home with tales of an "iron horse"—a steam-powered engine that could haul coal along metal rails. In 1828, America's first railroad company, the Baltimore and Ohio (B&O) began to build one of the country's first railways, linking Baltimore and Ellicott's Mills. The company

The B&O was the first railroad company in the United States.

also bought a steam engine able to reach a top speed of 20 miles (32 km) per hour. The engine made its first trip on August 28, 1830. As the locomotive belched black smoke and rattled down the track, passengers riding behind the engine thought the contraption might explode. Nicknamed Tom Thumb, this engine later ran a race with a horse to see if an iron horse could outrun a real one. A mechanical problem forced Tom Thumb out of the race, but it proved the day of steam and iron was at hand.

Race and War

The growth of the B&O expanded Maryland's role as a shipping and manufacturing center. In farming, the state also modernized, adopting new machinery and scientific methods to improve the harvest. But on tobacco farms in southern Maryland, little had changed. Slavery was still important to the farmers there; even more slaves worked as servants or in skilled trades, such as shipbuilding. No matter what their occupation, Maryland's blacks—slave and free—faced rigid racist attitudes.

By 1830, Maryland had almost 53,000 free blacks; most of them lived in Baltimore, where it was easier to find jobs than in smaller towns. The laws that affected blacks in Maryland continued to reflect the conflicting ideas on slavery and race relations that threatened to tear apart the country as a whole. In 1831, the state made it harder for slave owners to free their slaves. Other laws denied free blacks the right to vote or join the state militia.

A small group of Marylanders did vocally oppose slavery. Some were religious leaders who came to the state from the North. One abolitionist, or antislavery spokesman, was William Lloyd

Freedom Fighters

In the struggle to end slavery, Frederick Douglass (left) and Harriet Tubman (right) played major roles. As former slaves from Maryland, they knew first-hand the evils of that bondage.

Douglass was born in 1817 on a farm near Easton. He spent much of his youth in Baltimore, where he learned to read and write, which was highly unusual for a slave. In 1838, he escaped to Massachusetts and soon became a leading spokesman for the abolitionist movement. In his later years, Douglass held several government positions and pointed out the dangers of racism. "The life of the nation is secure," he said, "only while the nation is honest, truthful, and virtuous." Douglass died in 1895.

Tubman was born around 1820 on a plantation on the Eastern Shore. After she fled north to Philadelphia in 1849, Tubman returned often to the South to help lead other slaves to freedom. The secret organization that helped slaves escape was called the Underground Railroad, and Tubman was its most famous "conductor." On nearly 20 trips, she led about 300 slaves to their freedom. When fearful slaves changed their minds about fleeing, the strong-willed Tubman was known to point a gun at them and say, "Move or die."

During the Civil War, Tubman held a variety of jobs for the Union: nurse, scout, and spy. After the war, she helped build schools for the South's freed slaves. She continued to work for the rights of African-Americans until her death in 1913. ■

Garrison, who came to Baltimore in 1829. In a local paper, Garrison wrote, "Slavery is a monster, and he must be treated as such—hunted down bravely, despatched at a blow."

By 1860, the Southern states sensed that many Northerners wanted to end slavery. But the South relied on slaves to run its plantations and was not ready to see slavery end. After the election of President Abraham Lincoln, Southern states began to secede, or leave, the Union to form their own country—the Confederate States of America. As a slave state, Maryland was pressured by these states to secede. Many Marylanders wanted to join the new country, but other citizens, especially from the western part of the state, identified with the North. The state was pulled between the two sides, but Maryland remained a part of the United States.

Despite this official loyalty, individual Marylanders still showed their support for the South. On April 19, 1861, a Baltimore mob attacked troops from Massachusetts on their way to defend Washington, D.C. Four soldiers and twelve civilians died in the attack; they were the first casualties of the Civil War. About 22,000 Marylanders volunteered to fight for the South, and Union troops had to take over Baltimore to ensure its loyalty to the Union.

Life After the War

After the Civil War, most Marylanders were able to look beyond their divided support for the Union. The war ended slavery, but white Marylanders still had mixed feelings about blacks. The state refused to ratify the Fifteenth Amendment to the Constitution, which gave African-Americans the right to vote, and Maryland's freed blacks lacked legal equality. Still, some blacks, especially in

Fields of Blood

The Battle of Antietam was fought in Sharpsburg, Maryland, on September 17, 1862—the single bloodiest day of the Civil War. More than 23,000 Union and Confederate troops were killed or wounded during the fighting, part of General Robert E. Lee's plan to push his Southern troops into the North. Neither side won a clear victory, though the Union stopped Lee's advance. The battle inspired President Abraham Lincoln's Emancipation Proclamation, which freed the slaves in the South.

Today, Antietam is a National Battlefield, and thousands of visitors come to this quiet farmland that once rang with cannon fire and rifle shots. Off the main road is Miller's Cornfield, where some of the worst fighting took place. Another major battle came at Sunken Road, a narrow dirt lane that splits two fields. More than 5,000 casualties occurred at this spot, and soldiers nicknamed it "Bloody Lane." Antietam National Battlefield also has a cemetery where almost 5,000 Union troops are buried. ■

Baltimore, slowly began to enter professions such as law, education, and medicine, and to start their own businesses.

Industrial Growth—and Conflict

By the 1870s, Baltimore was a major industrial center. Its garment industry, dominated by German and Jewish immigrants, was a national leader. Local officials called Baltimore "the city that tries to suit everybody." Baltimore was also the canning capital of the country. Oysters, tomatoes, corn, and other produce were cooked and packed in cans to be shipped across the United States.

Shipping and train transportation remained important too, and by the 1870s the B&O Railroad linked the city with Chicago. Maryland's railroad workers were once called the "aristocrats of

First in the Nation

Going back to the eighteenth century, Baltimore was a city famous for introducing products and technology to America. Here are just some of the city's famous firsts:

1784 Thirteen-year-old Edward Warren takes the first hot-air balloon trip in America.

1817 Gas lamps light a street for the first time, in the Old Town section of Baltimore.

1828 The first umbrella factory opens, with the slogan, "Born in Baltimore, raised everywhere."

1844 "What hath God wrought" is the first message ever sent along the first telegraph line, which links Baltimore and Washington, D.C.

1851 Ice-cream maker Jacob Fussell introduces the first packaged carton of his cool treats.

1897 Simon Lake (right) invents the world's first practical submarine, the *Argonaut*. ■

labor," but in 1877 B&O workers grew unhappy with their low wages. A weak national economy forced the railroad to cut wages even further, and the workers went on strike. When strikers and their supporters rioted near Camden Station, one railroad official called the rioters "the fiercest mob ever known in Baltimore." State and federal troops ended the riots, but ten people died during the fighting. Maryland eventually passed laws to protect the rights of workers.

Riches from the Bay

Along Chesapeake Bay, fishing boomed like never before. The fishers were known locally as "watermen." While hauling huge nets through the bay, they often found crabs in their catch. Considered a nuisance, the crabs were usually crushed, but then some enterprising watermen realized that inside the crab's shell was a tasty meat, and another cash "crop" was born.

Oysters, however, remained the king of the Chesapeake. Sailing in local boats called bugeyes, watermen brought in about 10 million bushels of oysters a year. The record, set in 1884, was 15 million bushels. The Eastern Shore town of Crisfield became the center of the oyster industry, and women played a key role as shuckers—people who removed oysters from their shells. The oyster business was so profitable that Maryland and Virginia fishers often clashed over territorial boundaries between the two states. In the 1870s and 1880s, "oyster wars" featured raids on each other's oyster beds and the occasional exchange of gunfire.

With fishing on the Chesapeake, mining in the western corner, and farming scattered around the state, Maryland had a diverse,

successful economy at the end of the nineteenth century. Baltimore, though, remained the heart of business activity. By 1900, half the state's population lived in Baltimore. The city had one of the country's great universities, Johns Hopkins, as well as museums and green parks. Baltimore was a symbol of a modern Maryland, ready for the twentieth century.

CHAPTER FOUR

Troubles and Successes

The honk of a horn and the occasional smoky backfire of an engine announced the coming of a new era— the automobile age. The auto was important for Maryland, bringing new jobs and roads that linked the farthest corners of the state. Marylanders also took to another new form of transportation—the airplane. In 1910, half-a-million people attended a Baltimore air show. The next year, the U.S. government opened an airfield and training school at College Park. The exploits of pilots and planes thrilled the local residents, but soon the country would need those aircraft for World War I (1914–1918).

The Aberdeen Proving Ground opened during World War I.

"The War to End all Wars"

Even before the United States entered World War I in 1917, Maryland was preparing for war. In Baltimore, the Bethlehem Steel Company's shipyard turned out ships for the navy. On Chesapeake Bay, the state's oyster fleet helped patrol for German U-boats. The U.S. government chose sites in Maryland to train soldiers and prepare new weapons. Fort Meade opened in Anne Arundel County in 1917, and a marsh near Aberdeen became a weapons proving ground. In Edgewood, chemists developed deadly gases. Fort McHenry, the historic site of an earlier war, became a military hospital.

When the United States and its Allies won the war against Germany, Maryland celebrated along with the rest of the nation.

Opposite: Johns Hopkins University

But something seemed to be different. The modern world, according to one historian, had "left Marylanders searching for a moderate middle course between government control and liberty, conscience and tolerance, tradition and more progressive change."

Alcohol was one issue creating conflict in the state, and across the nation, too. Some religious leaders had struggled to prohibit the sale of alcohol since the nineteenth century, and a number of Eastern Shore counties had already gone "dry." The Eighteenth Amendment to the Constitution (adopted in 1919) made prohibition the law of the land, but many Marylanders refused to obey it, and Governor Albert C. Ritchie did not bother to enforce it. The state was known as the "wettest" in the country, and Maryland earned its nickname the "Free State" because it asserted its belief in individual freedom.

From a Roar to a Whimper

The prohibition era was known as "the Roaring Twenties." The country's economy grew and Americans looked for new ways to have fun: dancing the Charleston, watching "talkie" films, cheering on new sports heroes. Maryland shared in the good times. Baltimore became the third-largest exporting city in America, and more than 100 new factories opened.

But after almost a decade of fun and easy money, everything collapsed on October 24, 1929. The stock-market crash on New York's Wall Street wiped out the savings of people who had invested in stocks. Banks began to close as panicked people raced to withdraw their cash. By the next year, the country was in its worst economic crisis ever—the Great Depression.

ALL GAME. TO-DAY

The promenade at Ocean City was a popular place in the 1920s.

Some help came in 1933, when Franklin D. Roosevelt (FDR) assumed the presidency. He spent federal money on programs that created jobs and provided social benefits. Under one jobs program, former office workers from Baltimore labored in the hot sun building new streets. Given the tough times, the men were happy with any job. Other programs tried to help residents in the traditionally poor western and southern corners of the state. People from rural areas, especially blacks, flocked to Baltimore to look for work, often with little luck.

FDR's relief programs, known as the New Deal, didn't end the Depression, but they helped soften some of its worst effects. America's—and Maryland's—economy staggered through the 1930s.

The Other Clipper

In the nineteenth century, the Baltimore clipper was the pride of the city's shipyards. Fast and sleek, the clippers could outrun pirates or a threatening British warship with ease. In the twentieth century, Maryland introduced another famous clipper to the world. But it was wings and motors, not wind and sail, that made these clippers fly.

In 1929, airplane manufacturer Glenn Martin moved his company to the state. Soon after, Martin designed a new kind of plane with four engines. It could land and take off from the water and carry passengers across the ocean. His plane, the *China Clipper*, was named after the Baltimore sailing ships of old. The *China Clipper* began its maiden voyage on November 22, 1935, flying from San Francisco to the Philippines with stops along the way. Passengers ate off china plates inside the most luxurious airplane cabins of the day. The fare was $799 for a one-way ticket—was equal to about $10,000 today. ■

A New Kind of Town

During President Roosevelt's New Deal, the U.S. government experimented with new programs and ideas—including building a new town from scratch. Called Greenbelt, this planned community was built close to Washington, D.C. Construction began in 1936, as workers built almost 900 multi-family housing units. Stores, schools, and playgrounds rose up in the town, and everything was connected by sidewalks. About 5,000 people applied to live in Greenbelt, most of them government employees.

Critics said Greenbelt was too expensive to run, and the town had some problems. All the fish in the "swimming hole" died, and the water was not

very inviting for swimmers. Still, Greenbelt served as a model for another planned city. In the 1960s, using private investments, developer James

Rouse created Columbia. Located between Baltimore and Washington, Columbia is one of the most successful planned communities in America. ■

World War II (1939–1945)

On December 7, 1941, Japan launched a sneak attack on the U.S. naval base at Pearl Harbor, Hawaii. The next day, America declared war on Japan, formally entering World War II. (In Europe, the war had started in 1939 with Germany's invasion of Poland.) Just as they had during World War I, Marylanders eagerly contributed to the war effort.

Maryland's factories created many new products for the government. Chemical companies found a way to make the water stored on lifeboats drinkable for long periods of time. The Martin

During World War II, many women worked in factories to replace the men fighting in Europe.

airplane company manufactured military versions of its popular *China Clipper*. And Maryland's shipyards churned out ships at an amazing rate. Where it once took almost nine months to make a supply ship, workers were now able to build one every thirty days.

Individual Marylanders also played their part. Some 15,000 people volunteered to watch for enemy airplanes at spotting stations along the coast. More than 240,000 men and women served in the armed forces. At home, women took factory jobs to replace the men off fighting in Europe and the Pacific, and African-Americans found new job opportunities as well.

Changing Times

World War II boosted Maryland's population, as Americans came to the capital region to work for the government. Within a few years after the war ended in 1945, the state's economy was stronger than ever before. Housing boomed as new suburbs sprang up outside

Crusader for Justice

The great-grandson of a slave, Thurgood Marshall was born in Baltimore in 1908 and graduated from Howard University Law School. In 1935, while working for the National Association for the Advancement of Colored People (NAACP), he won a case that ended segregation at the University of Maryland School of Law. Marshall continued to argue—and win—major decisions in front of the U.S. Supreme Court. His biggest victory came in 1954, in *Brown* v. *Board of Education*. In that case, Marshall argued that "separate but equal" schooling was unconstitutional. The court agreed, and segregation laws began to fall.

In 1967, Marshall came to the Supreme Court again, but this time he was on the other side of the bench. President Lyndon B. Johnson named him the first African-American justice of the Supreme Court. Serving for twenty-four years, Marshall was known for his strong views on civil rights and freedom of speech. Marshall died in 1993. A memorial in Annapolis honors this Maryland native's lifelong dedication to equal justice for all. ■

Baltimore and Washington, D.C. Former soldiers put down their guns and picked up books, attending college under the GI Bill, which paid for their schooling. But things were not perfect—racism continued to make many of Maryland's African-Americans second-class citizens. The civil rights movement, which began in the 1950s, focused lasting attention on segregation across America and within Maryland.

Education was a major issue. Black children attended segregated schools that lacked the books and equipment found in Maryland's schools for whites. A Maryland native, attorney Thurgood Marshall, led the legal battle that finally ended school seg-

A Woman's Place Is in the Lab

Baltimore's Johns Hopkins University opened in 1876 and developed one of the finest medical schools and hospitals in America. Women, however, had a difficult time entering the school until the early twentieth century. One of the school's most famous early female graduates—and teachers—was Dr. Helen Taussig.

In 1930, Taussig became head of Johns Hopkins's pediatric heart clinic. She studied a fatal birth defect that caused a lack of oxygen in the blood. Babies born with the defect turned a light shade of blue. While examining these so-called blue babies, Taussig discovered that a faulty blood vessel in the heart caused the lack of oxygen. In 1944, she and Dr. Alfred Blalock developed the Blalock-Taussig technique, a surgical procedure that repaired the blood vessel. The operation saved thousands of lives and led to further advancements in heart surgery.

Taussig later became the first woman named a full professor at Johns Hopkins. She also led the fight against thalidomide, a drug that caused birth defects when taken by pregnant women. Taussig retired from Johns Hopkins in 1963 but continued medical research for many years. She died in 1986. ∎

regation in 1954. But the fight for total equality was not over. In 1968, after the assassination of civil rights leader Reverend Martin Luther King Jr., violent riots broke out in Baltimore. But Maryland was slowly beginning to fully integrate blacks into white society, giving them new economic and social opportunities.

Building for the Future

In the 1960s and 1970s, Maryland's economy turned to high-tech industries. Computers and medical research were especially important. The federal government funded much of the research in these areas and built the Goddard Space Flight Center in Greenbelt. The space center was a modern link to Maryland's long past as a home for innovations in transportation.

In Baltimore, however, things were not as promising. Manufacturers left the city, eliminating jobs. The harbor area, once a center of activity, was almost in ruins. In 1964, voters approved funding for a bold, long-term plan to rejuvenate the Inner Harbor. Corporations began building new headquarters near the water, and in 1980, Harborplace opened for business. This attractive retail center, with glass-encased walkways, attracted tourists to Maryland like never

Harborplace played a part in revitalizing Baltimore.

PEARL FAYE

Still Under Sail

Modern Maryland keeps close ties to its sailing heritage. Maryland's fishing fleet is the only one in the country still powered by sail, and many fishers still use boats like those first developed in the state. Maryland's sailing history and its current nautical connections are the main attractions at the Chesapeake Bay Maritime Museum.

Located in St. Michaels on the Eastern Shore, the museum features historic boats and exhibits that trace the influence of the bay on Maryland life. Centuries ago, the region's Native Americans built log canoes, sometimes setting small fires inside the logs to hollow them out. European settlers used the basic log-canoe design

and added sails, creating a variety of new boats. In the museum's Oystering Building, crafters rebuild a skipjack, one of the boats found along the bay. The Maritime Museum also has an authentic 1879 lighthouse, showing how lighthouse keepers and their families lived in the age before automated lighthouses. ■

before. A new aquarium and other attractions soon followed. By the 1990s, Baltimore had regained some of its past bustle, offering hope to struggling cities across America that they could also rebuild and grow.

Maryland in the 1990s was one of the wealthiest states, and its economy at the end of the decade was thriving. Besides encouraging new growth, the state government was focusing on preserving Maryland's rural character and natural resources, such as Chesapeake Bay. In 1998, Governor Parris N. Glendening could proudly claim, "Our citizens enjoy enhanced security, and feel a renewed sense of optimism."

CHAPTER FIVE

From the Mountains to the Bay

With its history of balancing extremes and finding a middle way, it seems appropriate that Maryland is one of the "Middle Atlantic" states. Geographers have given this name to the region that includes New York, Pennsylvania, New Jersey, and Delaware. Like most of these states, Maryland borders the Atlantic Ocean—but just barely. Its Atlantic coastline is only 31 miles long (50 km), a sliver of land on the extreme eastern edge of the Eastern Shore. From these ocean waters to the western border, Maryland has a variety of landforms, wildlife, and climates.

Maryland comprises a variety of landforms.

The Land

Maryland covers 12,297 square miles (31,849 sq km), including 680 square miles (1,761 sq km) of inland waters. It ranks forty-second in size among the fifty states. To the north, on the other side of Mason and Dixon's Line, is Pennsylvania. Mason and Dixon's Line then cuts south at Maryland's northeast corner to form the border with Delaware. The Potomac River, which starts its wind-

Opposite: Backpacking on the Appalachian Trail

Surveying the Wilderness

For decades, the Calverts of Maryland and the Penns of Pennsylvania could not agree on the border that separated their colonies. At one point in the 1730s, settlers in the two colonies clashed over the position of the boundary. Finally, in 1760, representatives from the two famous families agreed on a border. Three years later, wanting the border officially mapped, they hired "two persons who . . . are well-skilled in astronomy, mathematicks and surveying"—Charles Mason and Jeremiah Dixon.

Mason was about 35 years old at the time, and Dixon was 30. Both lived in England, where they were known for their scientific skills. They began their task in 1763. Mason and Dixon started by marking the border between Maryland and what is now Delaware, but which then belonged to Pennsylvania. Every 5 miles (8 km) they placed a stone. Carved into the side of the stone facing Maryland was the Calvert family crest, or emblem; the Penn crest was on the other side.

Mason and Dixon worked until December 1767, taking their line along the northern edge of Maryland into the Allegheny Mountains. The two scientists, used to a quiet life in the English countryside, traveled with Native American guides—and worried about meeting less friendly Indians. They also survived winter storms and wild animals.

Years after this surveying trip, Mason and Dixon's Line became known as the approximate geographic dividing line between the North and the South of the United States. ■

ing path to Chesapeake Bay in the Allegheny Mountains, separates Maryland from West Virginia and Virginia. Maryland's longest distance from east to west is 238 miles (383 km), along its border with Pennsylvania. From north to south the greatest distance is 125 miles (201 km), through the Eastern Shore. In the extreme western part of the state, in Washington County, the distance from the Pennsylvania border to West Virginia shrinks in some places to just a few miles.

Geographers divide Maryland into three main land regions: the Appalachian Mountains, the Piedmont Plateau, and the Atlantic Coastal Plain. The Appalachian Region is sometimes divided further, into the Appalachian Ridge and Valley and the Blue Ridge. Within these regions, Maryland shares geographic features with its neighboring states, but it also has unique features that shape Maryland's natural beauty.

The Appalachian Mountains

The Appalachians stretch from Alabama to Maine, and a number of smaller mountain ranges make up this long system, including the Alleghenies and the Blue Ridge Mountains. Both of these ranges cut through the western corner of Maryland. Some rock formations in the region date back more than 350 million years, and Maryland's tallest mountain peak, the 3,360-foot (1,025-m) Backbone Mountain, is in the Alleghenies. Before European settlers came to

South Mountain is one of Maryland's peaks within the Appalachian Mountains.

the area, Native Americans found a path through the mountains. Now known as Cumberland Narrows, this 1,000-foot (300-m) high gap let pioneers move farther west through the Alleghenies. The Blue Ridge, east of the Alleghenies, runs from south to north. Catoctin Mountain and South Mountain are two of Maryland's major peaks in this range.

The Appalachian region is the source of Maryland's coal, although this natural resource is not as plentiful here as it is in the mountains of neighboring Pennsylvania and West Virginia. The region, however, is not all mountains and ridges. Maryland's west-

Maryland's Geographical Features

Total area; rank	12,297 sq. mi. (31,849 sq km); 42nd
Land; rank	9,775 sq. mi. (25,317 sq km); 42nd
Water; rank	2,522 sq. mi. (6,532 sq km); 16th
Inland water; rank	680 sq. mi. (1,761 sq km); 31st
Coastal water; rank	1,842 sq. mi. (4,771 sq km); 4th
Geographic center	Prince Georges, 4.5 miles (7.24 km) northwest of Davidsonville
Highest point	Backbone Mountain, 3,360 feet (1,025 m)
Lowest point	Sea level along the coast
Largest city	Baltimore
Population; rank	4,798,622 (1990 census); 19th
Record high temperature	109°F (43°C) in Allegany County on July 3, 1898, and at Cumberland and Frederick on July 10, 1936
Record low temperature	–40°F (–40°C) at Oakland on January 13, 1912
Average July temperature	75°F (24°C)
Average January temperature	33°F (1°C)
Average annual precipitation	43 inches (109 cm)

The north branch of the Potomac River

ern corner also has rolling plateaus and green valleys. The Hagerstown Valley stands out as a prime agricultural area. The region's orchards contribute greatly to Maryland's fruit harvest.

The Potomac River flows along the Appalachian region's southern edge, and the Monocacy runs southward along the Blue Ridge into the Potomac. Melting snows from Backbone Mountain flow into the rugged Youghiogheny River—called the "Yock" by locals—famous for its white-water rapids. The Appalachian region also has a number of freshwater lakes—all artificially created. The state's deepest lake, Deep Creek Lake, is located in the Alleghenies.

Year-Round Resort

Deep Creek flows through Garrett County, a small triangle of land near the West Virginia border. In 1924, a power company built a dam on the creek to generate electricity. In the process, Maryland's largest freshwater lake was formed.

More than 2,400 feet (731 m) above sea level, Deep Creek Lake covers 3,900 acres (1,580 ha). The lake is 12 miles (19 km) long, with a shoreline that runs for 65 miles (105 km). Its average depth is 26.5 feet (8 m); it plunges to 72 feet (22 m) at its deepest point. Deep Creek Lake was leased to the state in 1980 to be used as a recreation area.

In summer, visitors come to enjoy the area's cool mountain temperatures and the lake's sparkling waters. People cruise the lake on every kind of craft, from canoes and paddleboats to powerboats and jet-skis. In winter, snowfalls that average 80 inches (203 cm) draw skiers to Wisp Resort, Maryland's only ski peak. ■

Piedmont Plateau

Piedmont is French for "foot of the mountain" and the Piedmont Plateau stretches for hundreds of miles, from New York to Alabama along the foot of the Appalachians. In Maryland, the plateau cuts through the center of the state, separating the mountainous region to the west and the low coastal plain to the east. The plateau has farmland and forests, with some hilly ranges up to 1,200 feet high (366 m) scattered around them. Frederick County, which straddles the Appalachian and Piedmont regions, has more farms than any other county in Maryland and is the state's center for dairy farming.

Heading east across the Piedmont, the land starts to flatten. The line that separates the plateau from the low coastal plain is called the Fall Line. At this point, with the change from steep land to flat, the rivers plunge down and form waterfalls. The roaring energy of some of these falls is used to generate electrical power. In Mary-

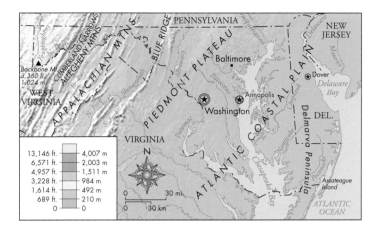

land, the Fall Line runs from the Great Falls of the Potomac, about 15 miles (24 km) northwest of Washington, D.C., northward to Elkton, near the Delaware border. Other rivers of the region include the Patapsco and the Patuxent, the longest river completely within Maryland.

A Recognized River

Most Americans probably know the Potomac River as the waterway that borders Washington, D.C., but the Potomac has special importance to Maryland. The state's first settlers sailed up this river after they entered Chesapeake Bay. The Indians along its banks called the river the Patawomeck. George Washington was born along the banks of the Potomac and was later buried near it, at Mount Vernon.

At 287 miles (462 km), the Potomac was used as a transportation route for passengers and goods. It is not one of America's longest rivers, but its significance was recognized by the U.S. government in 1998. The Potomac was one of fifteen rivers selected by the president to be listed as an "American Heritage River," reflecting its historical and cultural importance to the country. ■

The Atlantic Coastal Plain

Crossing the Fall Line leads to the Atlantic Coastal Plain, Maryland's largest land region. This area, which makes up more than half the state, is also known as the Tidewater Plain. Along with its flat lands, suitable for raising a variety of crops, the coastal plain is dotted with marshes and swamps. The Chesapeake Bay, with its Western and Eastern Shores, dominates the coastal plain.

The Eastern Shore is part of the Delmarva Peninsula, a name that comes from combining letters from each of the three states on the peninsula—*Del*aware, *Mar*yland, and *V*irgini*a*. The Chesapeake separates the Eastern Shore from the rest of Maryland, and for many years the region's inhabitants had a distinct sense of being distant—and different—from the rest of the state. On both shores, the Chesapeake has a number of small bays and inlets, and the water has both commercial and recreational uses. Important rivers of the region include the Susquehanna, which empties into the Chesapeake at Havre de Grace and contributes half of the bay's freshwater, and the Choptank and Nanticoke on the Eastern Shore.

The Delightful Bay

Early settler Father Andrew White called Chesapeake Bay "the most delightful water I ever saw." The bay is actually what scientists call a drowned riverbed. About 10,000 years ago, when the glacial ice melted, it pushed the Atlantic Ocean up and into the riverbed of the Susquehanna River.

Chesapeake Bay covers 3,237 square miles (8,384 sq km), with almost half in Virginia. It is 193 miles (311 km) long and 3 to 25 miles (5 to 40 km) wide. Although deep enough to accept large oceangoing vessels, the bay also has more than 1,000 square miles (2,590 sq km) under 6 feet (1.8 m) deep.

The bay's name comes from the Algonquin Indian word *Chesepiuk,* which was the name of an Indian village on the mouth of the bay. Some people have suggested that *Chesapeake* means "great saltwater" or "great shellfish bay," but no existing records support that claim. ■

Chesapeake Bay is a dominant part of the coastal plain.

Threats to the Chesapeake

Pollution in the Chesapeake Bay is not new. Harmful chemicals in products made by humans, such as fertilizers and soap, have been washed into the bay for years. The pollution levels hit their peak in the 1970s. At that time, the federal government and the states around the bay began to find better ways to keep pollutants out of the water. Now, however, the Chesapeake faces a new threat.

During the 1990s, a deadly microscopic organism called *Pfiesteria pisicicda* began to kill fish in the bay and sicken people exposed to it. Outbreaks of *Pfiesteria* led Maryland officials to close fishing areas on rivers near the bay. The *Pfiesteria* outbreak also caused some people to think all seafood from the bay was tainted, and it kept many tourists from visiting the scenic towns of the Eastern Shore.

In 1998, the Maryland government passed a law designed to reduce a possible source of the pollution that promotes the growth of *Pfiesteria*—nutrients in chicken manure. The manure is used to fertilize crops, and then the nutrients wash into the bay. Scientists are working to see if those nutrients are the cause of this environmental dilemma. ■

Maryland's Wildlife

With land that shifts from mountains to coastal shores, it's not surprising that Maryland has many species of plants and animals within its borders. About 2.7 million acres (1.1 million ha)—approximately 40 percent of Maryland's land area—is covered with forests. Trees include spruce, hemlock, white pine, and maple in the mountains and on the plateau. Pine and oak are found in the coastal region, and cypress grows along the bay.

A variety of mammals are found throughout the state, such as white-tailed deer, foxes, raccoons, rabbits, skunks, and woodchucks. Larger animals, such as buffalo and elk, once roamed the lands near Chesapeake Bay, but they no longer live in the state. One endangered species that lives along the bay is the Delmarva fox squirrel.

Maryland has a number of songbirds in its many forests, including the state's official bird, the Baltimore oriole. Maryland is also home to some rare birds, such as the endangered peregrine falcon and America's national symbol, the bald eagle. Perhaps the state's most famous flyers are the waterfowl and waterbirds along the Chesapeake. The fowl include a variety of ducks, such as canvasback, teal, and mallard. Canada geese and other northern birds spend their winters in Maryland. Waterbirds include elegant herons, egrets, and osprey, also known as water hawks.

Maryland's rivers and lakes contain a number of freshwater fish, such as trout and catfish. The waters of the Chesapeake, the state's best-known fishing grounds, are home to a variety of fish and shellfish. The most famous are the blue crabs, oysters, and clams so important to

An osprey returning to its nest

What's a Terp?

Sports fans may know that the University of Maryland athletic teams are nicknamed the Terrapins or Terps, but they might not know exactly what a terrapin is. The diamondback terrapin is a sea turtle native to the Chesapeake Bay. Averaging under 12 inches (30 cm) in length, terrapins are descendants of reptiles that lived more than 200 million years ago.

In Maryland, terrapins were once hunted for their meat, an ingredient in terrapin stew. In some places, terrapin "farmers" even raised the turtles in pens. Crisfield seafood packers once shipped terrapin meat around the world. Their popularity in stew almost made terrapins extinct, but Maryland passed laws to help preserve them. Today, wild terrapins leave their tracks on the beaches of the Eastern Shore. ■

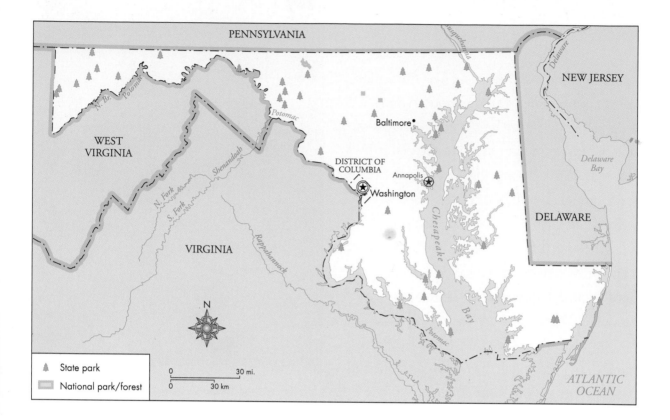

PENNSYLVANIA

Susquehanna

NEW JERSEY

Delaware

WEST
VIRGINIA

N. Br. Potomac

Potomac

Baltimore

Delaware
Bay

DISTRICT OF
COLUMBIA

Shenandoah

Annapolis

Washington

Chesapeake

DELAWARE

N. Fork

S. Fork

VIRGINIA

Rappahannock

Bay

N

Potomac

ATLANTIC
OCEAN

▲ State park

■ National park/forest

0   30 mi.

0   30 km

Maryland's parks and forests

Maryland commerce—and cooking. Another favorite fish is the striped bass, Maryland's state fish. Also called a rockfish, it's a prized catch for sports fishers.

Climate

Maryland's climate is as diverse as its wildlife. In the Appalachians, summers are cool, with average temperatures in July at 68°F (20°C). On the bay, summer temperatures average about 75°F (24°C). The eastern half of the state is warmed by the Gulf Stream, and summers can be sticky with high humidity. That warm climate, however, also means winters are less fierce in the east; temperatures average about 39°F (4°C), while the mountains have an average

winter temperature of 29°F (−2°C). Snowfall along the bay averages just around 10 inches (25 cm) per year, compared to about 80 inches (203 cm) in the mountains.

Snowfall can be plentiful in the mountain regions.

Maryland's Wild Ponies

As the wind sweeps across sandy dunes, small herds of wild ponies munch on the marsh grass that surrounds them. These ponies live on Assateague Island, a thin barrier of land between the Eastern Shore and the Atlantic Ocean. Two-thirds of the 37-mile (59.5-km)-long island belongs to Maryland, the rest to Virginia.

The ponies are the most famous inhabitants of Assateague Island National Seashore. There are no people there, and the island has no paved roads. Legends say the first ponies swam ashore from a sixteenth-century Spanish shipwreck. Actually, today's ponies are more likely the descendants of horses that were hidden on the island in the seventeenth century so that their owners wouldn't have to pay taxes on them. ■

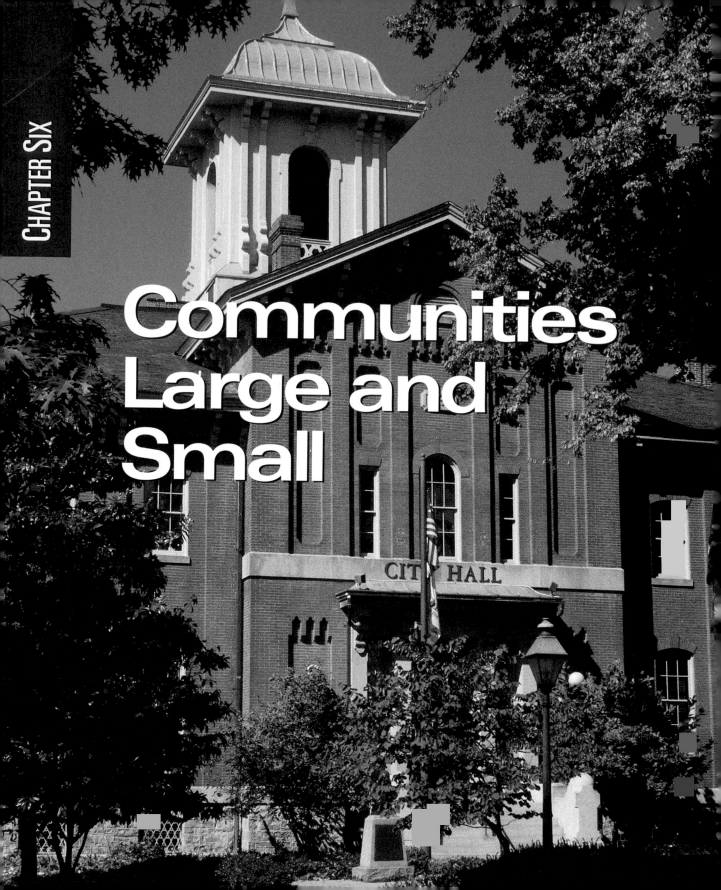

CHAPTER SIX

Communities Large and Small

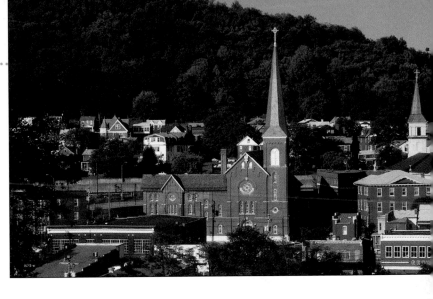

Maryland's approximately 5 million citizens live in a number of cities and towns spread across the state. Baltimore is the largest city, while some towns along the Eastern Shore have just a handful of families. Maryland's communities are as diverse as the state itself. They're filled with natural beauty, historic landmarks, and people who love the charms of their home state.

Cumberland is Maryland's western-most city

Cumberland

The state's major westernmost city, Cumberland, lies in Maryland's thin, mountainous panhandle. Established in 1785, Cumberland grew as a major transportation center for goods and for settlers heading into west. Before then, the city was the site of Fort Cumberland, where a young George Washington served as commander during the French and Indian War. The cabin where he lived still stands in the city.

In 1806, Congress authorized the country's first national highway, the National Road, to connect Cumberland to Wheeling, Virginia. An earlier road had already linked Cumberland to Baltimore. Cumberland was also the final destination on the Chesapeake and Ohio Canal, a 184-mile (296-km) canal between the western city and Georgetown, in the District of Columbia. The Chesapeake and Ohio Canal National Historical Park re-creates a slice of life along the canal, which was completed in 1850 and used until

Opposite: City Hall in Frederick

Hager and His Town

Like many eighteenth-century German immigrants to Maryland, Jonathan Hager settled in the western part of the colony. In 1737, he bought 200 acres (81 ha) of land and named his farm "Hager's Fancy." When he married his wife, Elizabeth, the next year, he built their new home above two springs, guaranteeing a protected supply of fresh-water. Other settlers came to the region and, like Hager, many named their property. Some of the more unusual names were "Near the Navel," "Trouble Enough," and "The Widow's Last Shift." The town that developed around Hager and his neighbors was known as Elizabeth Town, for his wife. In 1814, the name was changed to Hagerstown.

Jonathan Hager became a successful trader, farmer, and gunsmith. Hager also served in the Maryland General Assembly and was a strong supporter of colonial rights. However, he didn't get a chance to fight for American independence; he died in 1775 while helping to build a church on land he had donated. ■

1924. Just outside Cumberland is the Paw Paw Tunnel, a 3,118-foot (946-m)-long tunnel cut through the mountains for the canal. Its construction was an engineering marvel for the era.

Frederick

In the heart of prime farmland and horse country, Frederick has been called the "gateway to western Maryland." The city's beautifully preserved eighteenth- and nineteenth-century buildings hint at its historical importance. Francis Scott Key was born nearby and is buried in Frederick's Mount Olivet Cemetery. Key practiced law in Frederick with his sister's husband, Roger Brooke Taney, who later became the chief justice of the U.S. Supreme Court. Taney's house features exhibits on both of these famous Frederick men.

Frederick's most famous woman is undoubtedly Barbara Fritchie. In 1862, according to local legend and a poem by John Greenleaf Whittier, Fritchie confronted Confederate general Stonewall Jackson and his troops as they were about to shoot a U.S. flag. "Shoot if you must this old grey head," Fritchie says in the poem, "but spare your country's flag." Fritchie's heroics are stirring, but historians agree they probably never happened. Still, her home—a replica of the original, which was destroyed in a flood—is a popular tourist attraction.

Just outside Frederick is Monocacy National Battlefield. Less well known than nearby Antietam, Monocacy was the site of a small but important battle. Union troops held off Southern forces long enough for General Ulysses S. Grant to send Northern reinforcements to Washington, D.C., preserving the safety of the nation's capital.

Also near Frederick, in the Catoctin Mountains, is the presidential retreat called Camp David. This secluded retreat built for U.S. presidents was first used by Franklin Delano Roosevelt, who called it Shangri-La. In 1953, President Dwight D. Eisenhower renamed it in honor of his grandson.

Barbara Fritchie confronting Stonewall Jackson and his army

President and Mrs. Bush at Camp David

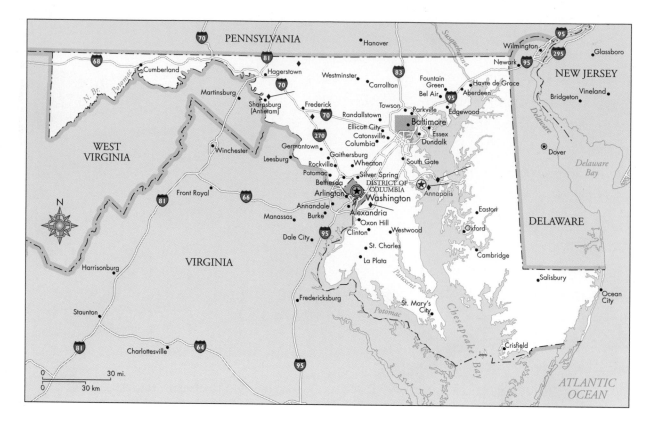

The Capital Region

Frederick County marks the northern tip of what is sometimes called the Capital Region—the Maryland cities and suburbs that ring Washington, D.C. Silver Spring is the largest of these communities. Rockville, the region's major city, has many well-preserved, stately old buildings, such as the Beall-Dawson House, which dates from 1815. The small town of Glen Echo has a tribute to Clara Barton, founder of the American Red Cross. Barton spent her last years in town at a house that is now a National Historic Site.

With Washington, D.C., so close by, it's not surprising that the federal government has a large presence in this part of Maryland. The nation's major medical research agency, the National Institutes of Health, has its headquarters in Bethesda. The NASA/Goddard

Andrews Air Force Base is one example of the federal government's presence in Maryland.

Space Flight Center, in Greenbelt, tracks the Hubble Space Telescope and U.S. satellites orbiting Earth. Andrews Air Force Base, the home of the president's plane, *Air Force One*, is located in Prince George's County, just outside Washington.

A Deadly Conspiracy

On April 14, 1865, America's most-wanted criminal crept up to a tavern in Clinton, Maryland. John Wilkes Booth had just shot and killed President Abraham Lincoln, and now he was stopping at the house of Mary Surratt (right), where he had stored weapons and supplies for his escape.

Mary's son, John, had planned with Booth to kidnap Lincoln, and he remained part of the conspiracy when the mission changed to murder. Booth, Surratt, and the others involved in the plot met at Mary Surratt's house—though she was not actually in on the plans. Even so, after the assassination she was convicted and executed—the first woman ever executed by the federal government.

Surratt's Tavern is just one of several Maryland landmarks associated with Lincoln's assassination. Near La Plata, in southern Maryland, was the home of Dr. Samuel Mudd, the doctor who set the leg Booth broke when he jumped from Lincoln's balcony in Ford's Theater. Booth himself was a Maryland native, born in Fountain Green, a small town outside of Bel Air. He is buried in Baltimore's Green Mount Cemetery. ■

Tobacco is a primary crop in the state's southern region.

Tobacco Country

Since colonial days, southern Maryland has been the state's prime tobacco-growing region. For many years, one of the major towns was Port Tobacco, but surprisingly, it was not named for that leafy crop. The name comes from a local Indian tribe, the Potobac, who lived in the area. Early Marylanders turned Port Tobacco into a bustling commercial center, but the town virtually disappeared after the harbor filled with silt and the county seat was moved to La Plata. Today, Port Tobacco and the surrounding area provide a sense of Maryland's "Old South" roots, with plantations and a relaxed lifestyle.

At the southernmost tip of the Western Shore is Point Lookout. During the Civil War, the North forced Confederate soldiers to a

The First Stop

St. Mary's City, at the southern tip of the Western Shore, was Maryland's first permanent town and capital. But before Leonard Calvert and his party built their fort there, they came ashore at St. Clement's Island.

Located in the Potomac River, St. Clement's is just a speck of land, covering about 60 acres (24 ha). On St. Clement's, Father Andrew White said a Mass of thanksgiving—the first Roman Catholic Mass held in America—and Leonard Calvert read the charter granted to his brother Cecilius, Lord Baltimore. Calvert took "solemne possession of the Country" for his family.

St. Clement's can be reached only by boat. The island features a 40-foot (12-m) concrete cross that honors Calvert's landing and a museum dedicated to the Potomac River and the local region. ■

prisoner-of-war camp at this remote spot. The camp was the largest in the North. Out of the 52,000 Confederate soldiers who were held there, more than 4,000 prisoners died.

The Capital City

Annapolis became Maryland's capital in 1695. First settled in 1649, the town was then called Providence. Annapolis is sometimes called "a museum without walls" because of the many well-preserved buildings that line its brick streets. In 1769, an English visitor to Annapolis predicted, "In a few years, it will probably be one of the best built cities in America." Today, the town's historic dis-

Annapolis is rich with history and beautiful views.

trict has more than 1,500 buildings, including more from the eighteenth century than any other town in America.

Annapolis's most famous site is the Maryland State House, America's oldest state capitol in continuous use. Construction of the present building was started in 1772. The building was capped with the largest wooden dome in the country. Made from cypress, the dome is held together with wooden pegs.

From November 1783 to August 1784, Annapolis served as the nation's capital, and the Continental Congress met at the Maryland State House. A crowd gathered in the Senate Chambers on December 23, 1783, where George Washington resigned as commander-in-chief of the Continental Army. "Many of the spectators," one congressman noted, ". . . shed tears on this solemn and affecting occasion." Just a few weeks later, the Treaty of Paris, which officially ended the American Revolution, was signed in that same room.

Three of Maryland's signers of the Declaration of Independence came from Annapolis. William Paca built a house in the 1760s, with 37 rooms and a grand 2-acre (0.8-ha) garden with terraces, a pond, and a summerhouse. Another signer, Samuel Chase, began building the Chase-Lloyd House in 1769. The only Catholic to sign the Declaration, Charles Carroll, was born in Annapolis, and his home is also open to the public.

Although filled with great homes of the past, Annapolis is now the home of thou-

A dress parade at the U.S. Naval Academy

An Early Navy Hero

The U.S. Naval Academy has a building known as the Chapel (right). That simple name, however, does not indicate the magnificence of this domed cathedral, with its soaring ceilings and stained-glass windows. Almost as impressive is a room underneath the cathedral—the crypt of John Paul Jones.

Jones lived for a time in Virginia before joining the American struggle for independence as a sea captain. In 1779, while commanding the *Bonhomme Richard*, he uttered his famous line, "I have not yet begun to fight!" Jones and his crew defeated the British warship *Serapis* in one of history's great naval battles.

Jones died in France in 1792 and was buried in a Paris cemetery. More than 100 years later, an American diplomat found his grave and arranged to have Jones's remains brought to Annapolis and buried beneath the Naval Academy Chapel. ■

sands of special guests—the men and women of the U.S. Naval Academy. The academy has trained America's naval officers since its founding in 1845. The school takes advantage of Annapolis's excellent port location, where the Severn River meets the Chesapeake. About 4,000 students—called midshipmen—live on the campus in one of the world's largest dormitories, Bancroft Hall. The building has 33 acres (13 ha) of floor space and 5 miles (8 km) of hallways.

City of Many Names

Annapolis is the political center of Maryland, but Baltimore, just 25 miles (40 km) to the north, is its one true metropolis. Baltimore is one of America's largest ports and a major commercial center. It has museums and performance centers, universities, sports facilities—all the public buildings that mark a modern city. But most important, Baltimore has a rich mix of people, and the city's many

Park near Baltimore harbor

neighborhoods give it a warm, welcoming atmosphere, leading to one of its nicknames—"Charm City."

Instead of rows of high-rise towers, many streets have neat brick row houses, some with marble steps in front—a Baltimore trademark. Some neighborhoods are associated with particular ethnic or racial groups, such as Little Italy, just past the harbor, and West and Northwest Baltimore, the home of many African-Americans. Other neighborhoods are named for people, such as the harbor area of Fells Point. Federal Hill, overlooking the harbor, was named for a huge party held there in 1788 to celebrate the ratification of the U.S. Constitution. To the north, Roland Park is home to many of Baltimore's wealthiest citizens. An industrial part of the city is called Sparrows Point. Here, huge mills once turned out tons of steel every year. These and other neighborhoods have led some people to call Baltimore "the city of neighborhoods."

In 1904, many of those neighborhoods were destroyed in a huge fire that roared through the city. More than seventy city blocks were wiped out, and the orange glow of the fire could be seen in Washington, D.C. Amazingly, no one was killed, and afterward Baltimoreans rebuilt their city, putting in better roads and improving the harbor.

Making a Point

In 1726, three years before Baltimore was founded, Edward Fell settled east of Jones Falls, the waterfall that powered many of the town's early mills. In 1730, Edward was joined by his brother William, and the land they owned was called Fell's Point. This early community eventually became part of Baltimore.

Other settlers came to the point, and many of them turned to shipbuilding. The harbor was the focus of activity in Fell's Point, and its shipyards produced Baltimore's famous clipper ships. Fell's Point also became a residential area, and in 1761 Edward Fell laid out a plan for the streets, giving many of them notable English names, such as Thames and Shakespeare. One nineteenth-century resident was Frederick Douglass, who worked in the shipyards while still a slave.

Over time, Fells Point lost the apostrophe in its name, but it retained its nautical atmosphere. Today, Fells Point attracts visitors with its many shops and restaurants (above), and the Broadway Market offers fresh produce for sale. More than 200 brick homes in the neighborhood built before the War of 1812 add to its charm. ■

Another Baltimore nickname is the "Monumental City," because of the many impressive monuments that dot the landscape. In 1815, the city began building the first major monument in memory of George Washington. Another monument, called Battle Monument, honors the citizens and soldiers killed during the Battle of Baltimore in 1814. The Francis Scott Key Monument celebrates the man who wrote "The Star-Spangled Banner" during that battle.

Three Brothers and their Mill

In 1772, Joseph, Andrew, and John Ellicott, three Quakers from Pennsylvania, bought 700 acres (283 ha) of land on the Patapsco River, just west of Baltimore. Two years later, after hauling their own equipment to the site, the brothers opened a flour mill. They built a road to bring their flour to Baltimore, and eventually their Patapsco flour was known across America. The Ellicotts' success helped end tobacco's role as the major cash crop in Maryland and increased the importance of growing and processing grains.

The town of Ellicott's Mills grew around the flour business and soon became a major industrial center. In 1830, the first B&O railway linked the town with Baltimore. Ellicott's Mills was later renamed Ellicott City. A flood in 1868 wiped out the flour mill; a plant for making doughnuts was later built in the area. Today, Ellicott City is a well-preserved example of a nineteenth-century mill town. ■

Monument to Francis Scott Key

Key and his accomplishment are an important part of Baltimore history. The original manuscript of his poem is on display at the Maryland Historical Society in the city, and Fort McHenry, where the famous battle took place, stands just south of the harbor.

Key was not the only writer associated with Baltimore. Two of America's greatest writers, H. L. Mencken and Edgar Allan Poe, lived in the city. Collections of their papers are stored at the Enoch Pratt Free Library, one of the largest public libraries in America, and Poe's house is open to the public. Other citizens and institutions in Baltimore have contributed greatly to American cultural life. Maryland's largest museum is the Baltimore Museum of Art, which features a large number of works by modern painters. The Peale Museum (now closed) was America's first planned museum building. It was founded by painter Rembrandt Peale in 1814, and two years later, the museum was lit by the first gaslights in Baltimore. Another city museum, the Great Blacks in Wax Museum, has wax sculptures of some of America's most famous African-Americans.

The USS *Constellation* is docked in Baltimore's Inner Harbor.

Baltimore's intellectual life is also stimulated by Johns Hopkins University, one of the finest colleges in the country. Johns Hopkins is world famous for its medical school and is the home of the Peabody Conservatory, the nation's oldest music school. The conservatory was named for George Peabody, a wealthy Baltimore banker of the nineteenth century.

Along with improving their minds, Baltimoreans like to have fun, and they have turned the Inner Harbor into an exciting mixture of attractions. Along the harbor is the shopping area called Harborplace; the Maryland Science Center, with hands-on exhibits for kids; and the National Aquarium. The USS *Constellation*, a nineteenth-century warship, underwent restoration in 1999 and now sits at the dock along with other historic ships, open to the public.

Salisbury

Across Chesapeake Bay on the Eastern Shore is a city almost as old as Baltimore, if not as big and famous. Located just south of Delaware, Salisbury sits on the banks of the Wicomico River. It's the only true city on the Eastern Shore and the business center for Maryland's poultry industry.

Salisbury did not share Baltimore's main advantage of a great natural port. Its harbor had to be dug out of the Wicomico River. And the city lacks some of the historic charm of other Maryland communities; fires in 1860 and 1886 destroyed most of its older buildings. But Salisbury is the commercial center of the Eastern Shore. Roads from Virginia and Delaware crossed here, and it developed the only major factories on Maryland's share of the

Delmarva Peninsula. Salisbury also has a zoo, considered one of the best small zoos in United States.

Crisfield

Farther south, at the tip of the Eastern Shore, is Crisfield. Called the "Seafood Capital of the World," Crisfield is a more typical Eastern Shore community than is Salisbury, as its nickname suggests. The town's fortunes are closely tied to the bay. Crisfield boomed around 1870, when a railroad was extended to a small town then known as Somers Cove. The trains and improved canning techniques made it easy to ship Chesapeake crabs and oysters across the country, and by 1900 the newly named town of Crisfield had more than 150 seafood-processing plants

Women have traditionally shucked oysters in Crisfield, and with amazing skill. One nineteenth-century observer noted how a Crisfield shucker ". . . inserts a thin knife between the shells, and with a quick turn of the wrist the shell is opened, the oyster cut loose and dropped into the pan, all in one movement."

Today, blue crabs—hard-shelled and soft-shelled—are Crisfield's major product. True to its roots, Crisfield holds two annual seafood festivals each summer.

Crisfield is known as the "Seafood Capital of the World."

Wye Mills

In the heart of the Eastern Shore is the small town of Wye Mills. The town has two famous landmarks. The Wye Mill, which dates from the seventeenth century, is Maryland's oldest commercial building in continuous operation. The mill once ground flour used by General Washington and his troops during the American Revolution, and its granite stones still grind corn and wheat today. Not far from the mill is the Wye Oak, the largest white oak in the country.

Glories of the Past

Today, the Eastern Shore town of Oxford is the home of watermen and Marylanders seeking a summer retreat. But for many years, Oxford was one of Maryland's most important ports. The town had already been settled for about twenty years when, in 1683, the Maryland General Assembly made Oxford and Annapolis Maryland's two ports of entry. All products shipped to and from the colony had to pass through one of these two ports. Surrounded by tobacco plantations, Oxford became a major shipping center.

Oxford continued to prosper until the Revolutionary War. After British ships left the region, businesses failed and people left town. Things were so quiet that cows could graze peacefully in the middle of the streets. But in the 1870s, just like Crisfield, Oxford benefited from a new railway and seafood-canning plants. The town bustled again until its oyster beds were picked clean. Then the trains left, the plants closed, and Oxford slumbered once more.

Tourists and recreational boaters have rediscovered Oxford's waterside charms and its historical past. The town was the home of some important Marylanders, including Matthew and Tench Tilghman. Matthew was a political leader at the time of the American Revolution. His son-in-law Tench served as General George Washington's aide. In 1781, Tench carried the news to the Continental Congress of England's surrender at the Battle of Yorktown. ■

CHAPTER SEVEN

Democracy in Action

I n 1776, shortly after Maryland's political leaders voted to join the cause for independence, they decided their newly free state needed a new kind of government. No longer controlled by either the Calverts or the English Crown, the leaders drew up a constitution for Maryland, outlining who could run for office and how laws would be made. Later, Marylanders helped the new United States make its Constitution too.

State and National Constitutions

The 1776 state constitution was what many people consider a conservative document. Despite taking the bold step of declaring independence from Britain, Maryland's leaders kept many of the old ways of doing things. Maryland already had a General Assembly with two houses, the Senate and the House of Delegates. Representatives in these houses made laws and the governor carried them out. This system did not change under the new constitution. Voters and officeholders had to own a certain amount of cash or property to participate in the political process. Women were excluded from public affairs, though free blacks were allowed to vote.

When the United States held its Constitutional Convention in 1787, Maryland sent five delegates. The most outspoken was Luther Martin, a lawyer who opposed any plans that seemed to

Women had to fight for their right to vote in Maryland as well as in the rest of the country.

Opposite: The State House in Annapolis

Maryland sent five delegates to the Constitutional Convention in 1787.

favor large states, such as Virginia, at the expense of smaller states, such as Maryland. Martin also wanted to limit the power of the federal government over the individual states and called for the protection of individual liberties. Many other politicians shared this last desire, and the Bill of Rights, the first ten amendments to the Constitution, was added to the original document.

A New and Troubled Era

As did many other states, Maryland slowly added democratic reforms to its original government. In 1837, voters were allowed to vote directly for state senators and the governor. Before then, these positions were filled after votes by members of the House of Delegates. A new constitution in 1851 created new government offices, and voters could directly elect certain public officials who once had been appointed by the governor or General Assembly.

A Taxing Case

In the early years of the Republic, Maryland's laws and the national government came into conflict. In 1816, Congress created a national bank. Two years later, Maryland placed a tax on any bank that was not chartered by the state's General Assembly, meaning the national bank. James McCulloch, the head of the Maryland branch of the national bank, refused to pay the tax. A Baltimore court upheld the state law, but when the case of *McCulloch* v. *Maryland* was appealed, the U.S. Supreme Court overturned the Maryland tax.

In a famous decision, Chief Justice John Marshall ruled that Maryland, and the other states, did not have the legal power to tax a federal institution, such as the national bank. The American people, Marshall wrote, "did not design to make their government dependent on the states." This case helped strengthen the authority of the national government versus the rights of states to do as they pleased. Maryland's loss was Washington, D.C.'s gain. ■

The 1851 constitution was drafted as slavery was becoming an emotional national issue. Most Marylanders were not ready to abolish slavery, but they ignored early talk of the South seceding from the Union.

When secession finally came in 1860, Maryland remained loyal to the Union, but reluctantly. Support for the South was widespread, but a new constitution adopted in 1864 abolished slavery in Maryland. After the Civil War, another new constitution undid many of the changes in the 1864 document. The constitution passed in 1867 remains in effect today, with a number of amendments added over the years.

The State Government Today

Just as the United States does, Maryland has three branches of government. The legislative branch makes the laws of the state. The laws are then carried out by the executive branch. The judicial

A bell from the USS Maryland is on the State House grounds.

The State Flag and Seal

Maryland's flag is a striking mix of colors and shapes. These images come from the coat of arms of the first Lord Baltimore, George Calvert. (A coat of arms is a symbol used by distinguished families.) The flag is divided into quarters, with the upper left and lower right quarters showing the Calverts' coat of arms in black and gold—now the state's official colors. The other two quarters, each with a red and white cross, show the coat of arms of the Crosslands, the family of Calvert's mother.

The design for the flag was taken from the state seal, which shows the Calvert and Crossland arms on a shield. Flags with this design were first flown in the late nineteenth century, and in 1904, the current flag was officially adopted as the state flag. Maryland was one of the first states to fly its own flag. ■

Maryland State Symbols

State bird: Baltimore oriole With its vibrant yellow-gold and black coloring, the Baltimore oriole nearly matches the Calvert family colors and was named for Lord Baltimore. In 1882, the state General Assembly gave the bird special protection, and sixty-five years later it named the Baltimore oriole the state bird.

State dog: Chesapeake Bay retriever In the early nineteenth century, this type of retriever was first bred in Maryland. The Chesapeake Bay retriever was named the state dog in 1964.

State fish: Striped bass The number of striped bass (also called rockfish) in the Chesapeake Bay was once on the decline, but efforts by Maryland and its neighbors on the bay have reduced pollution and helped the rockfish make a comeback. The striped bass was named Maryland's state fish in 1965.

State insect: Baltimore checkerspot butterfly Found all over Maryland, this butterfly is black with orange and white spots. The checkerspot was named the state insect in 1973.

State crustacean: Blue crab This popular shellfish, a symbol of the bounty of the Chesapeake Bay, was named the state crustacean in 1989.

State flower: Black-eyed Susan This black-and-gold flower (above), a type of daisy, blooms with the state's colors in July. The General Assembly made the black-eyed Susan the state flower in 1918.

State boat: Skipjack The skipjack is a sailing ship native to Maryland and used by watermen who dredge for oysters. Named for a kind of leaping fish, a skipjack has one mast and a V-shaped bottom. The General Assembly named it the state boat in 1985.

State tree: White oak Maryland's state tree is represented by one great example of the species, the Wye Oak (above right). Located at Wye Mills on the Eastern Shore, the Wye Oak is 96 feet (29 m) tall, and its branches extend 119 feet (36 m). The tree is thought to be almost 450 years old, and is one of the largest white oaks in the world. The white oak was named the state tree in 1941.

State sport: Jousting Maryland was the first state with an official sport, and it chose the medieval event of jousting (below). Today's jousters, however, don't wear armor or try to knock their opponents to the ground, as knights of old did. On horseback, a modern jouster uses a lance to spear rings of various sizes. Jousting became popular in Maryland during the nineteenth century and was named the state sport in 1962. ▪

Maryland's State Song

"Maryland, My Maryland"

On April 19, 1861, Northern troops marching through Baltimore battled local residents who supported the South. Maryland native James Ryder Randall heard about the killings while living in Louisiana, and he wrote a poem in support of the Confederacy. His poem was set to the music of "O, Tannenbaum" (also called "Oh, Christmas Tree"). "Maryland, My Maryland" became the state's official song in 1939.

The despot's heel is on thy shore, Maryland, my Maryland!
His torch is at thy temple door, Maryland, my Maryland!
Avenge the patriotic gore that flecked the streets of Baltimore,
and be the battle queen of yore, Maryland, my Maryland!

Hark to an exiled son's appeal, Maryland, my Maryland!
My mother state to thee I kneel, Maryland, my Maryland!
For life and death, for woe and weal, thy peerless chivalry reveal,
and gird thy beauteous limbs with steel, Maryland, my Maryland!

Thou wilt not cower in the dust, Maryland, my Maryland!
Thy gleaming sword shall never rust, Maryland, my Maryland!
Remember Carroll's sacred trust, remember Howard's warlike thrust,
And all thy slumb'rers with the just, Maryland, my Maryland!

branch is responsible for interpreting the laws and determining whether they are constitutional.

The executive branch is led by the governor, who serves a four-year term. No governor may serve more than two consecutive terms. The governor is aided by a lieutenant governor, the attorney general, the secretary of state, and various other officials and executive departments and commissions.

Maryland's legislative branch, called the General Assembly, is

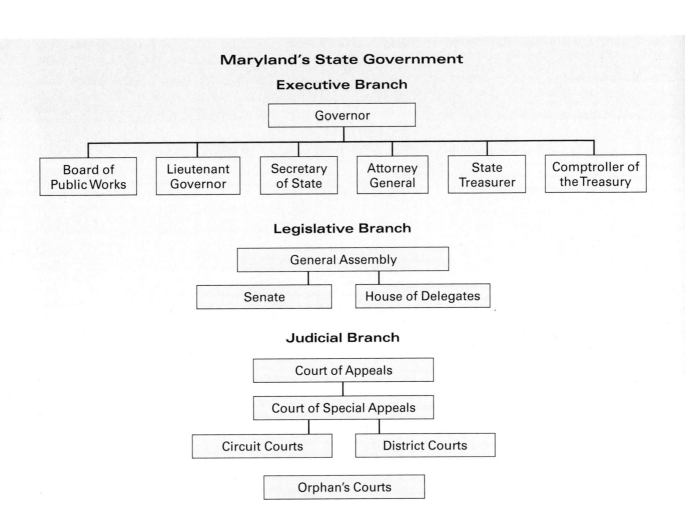

Maryland's State Government

Executive Branch

Governor

- Board of Public Works
- Lieutenant Governor
- Secretary of State
- Attorney General
- State Treasurer
- Comptroller of the Treasury

Legislative Branch

General Assembly

- Senate
- House of Delegates

Judicial Branch

Court of Appeals

Court of Special Appeals

- Circuit Courts
- District Courts

Orphan's Courts

split into the House of Delegates and the Senate. The House has 141 members; the Senate has 47. The state is divided into forty-seven legislative districts, and voters in each elect one senator and three delegates. All members serve four-year terms. The General Assembly meets at the State House in Annapolis every year on the second Wednesday in January and stays in session for ninety days.

Maryland's Governors

Name	Party	Term	Name	Party	Term
Thomas Johnson	None	1777–1779	Philip Francis Thomas	Dem.	1848–1851
Thomas Sim Lee	None	1779–1782	Enoch Louis Lowe	Dem.	1851–1854
William Paca	None	1782–1785	Thomas Watkins Ligon	Dem.	1854–1858
William Smallwood	None	1785–1788	Thomas Holliday Hicks	Know-Nothing	1858–1862
John Eager Howard	Fed.	1788–1791			
George Plater	Fed.	1791–1792	Augustus W. Bradford	Union	1862–1866
James Brice	Unknown	1792	Thomas Swann	Dem.	1866–1869
Thomas Sim Lee	Fed.	1792–1794	Oden Bowie	Dem.	1869–1872
John H. Stone	Fed.	1794–1797	William Pinkney Whyte	Dem.	1872–1874
John Henry	Fed.	1797–1798	James Black Groome	Dem.	1874–1876
Benjamin Ogle	Fed.	1798–1801	John Lee Carroll	Dem.	1876–1880
John Francis Mercer	Dem.-Rep.	1801–1803	William T. Hamilton	Dem.	1880–1884
Robert Bowie	Dem.-Rep.	1803–1806	Robert M. McLane	Dem.	1884–1885
Robert Wright	Dem.-Rep.	1806–1809	Henry Lloyd	Dem.	1885–1888
James Butcher	Unknown	1809	Elihu E. Jackson	Dem.	1888–1892
Edward Lloyd	Dem.-Rep.	1809–1811	Frank Brown	Dem.	1892–1896
Robert Bowie	Dem.-Rep.	1811–1812	Lloyd Lowndes	Rep.	1896–1900
Levin Winder	Fed.	1812–1816	John Walter Smith	Dem.	1900–1904
Charles Ridgely	Fed.	1816–1819	Edwin Warfield	Dem.	1904–1908
Charles Goldsborough	Fed.	1819	Austin L. Crothers	Dem.	1908–1912
Samuel Sprigg	Dem.-Rep.	1819–1822	Phillips Lee Goldsborough	Rep.	1912–1916
Samuel Stevens Jr.	Dem.-Rep.	1822–1826			
Joseph Kent	Dem.	1826–1829	Emerson C. Harrington	Dem.	1916–1920
Daniel Martin	Anti-Jackson	1829–1830	Albert C. Ritchie	Dem.	1920–1935
Thomas King Carroll	Dem.	1830–1831	Harry W. Nice	Rep.	1935–1939
Daniel Martin	Anti-Jackson	1831	Herbert R. O'Conor	Dem.	1939–1947
			Wm. Preston Lane Jr.	Dem.	1947–1951
George Howard	Anti-Jackson	1831–1833	Theodore R. McKeldin	Rep.	1951–1959
James Thomas	Anti-Jackson	1833–1836	J. Millard Tawes	Dem.	1959–1967
			Spiro T. Agnew	Rep.	1967–1969
Thomas W. Veazey	Whig	1836–1839	Marvin Mandel	Dem.	1969–1979
William Grason	Dem.	1839–1842	Blair Lee III (acting gov.)	Dem.	1977–1979
Francis Thomas	Dem.	1842–1845	Harry R. Hughes	Dem.	1979–1987
Thomas G. Pratt	Whig	1845–1848	William D. Schaefer	Dem.	1987–1995
			Parris N. Glendening	Dem.	1995–

Troubled Governor

Maryland's past governors include William Paca, a signer of the Declaration of Independence, and Albert Ritchie, who was considered a possible presidential candidate in the 1920s. But the only governor to move on to high national office was Spiro Agnew (right). His term, however, ended in disappointment for the Marylanders he once served.

Born in 1918, Agnew was the son of a Greek immigrant who ran a Baltimore diner. After serving in World War II, Agnew studied law. He didn't enter politics until 1962, when he won the post of county executive for Baltimore County. Four years later, the Republican lawyer was elected governor of the state.

Agnew served during troubled times. Racial violence was erupting across Maryland and the country. Agnew tried to calm the tensions, while not tolerating illegal acts. He also tried to integrate the government, naming the first African-American to a high state position. In 1968, Richard Nixon chose Agnew to be his vice president, saying he had a "quiet confidence about him."

Once in office, Vice President Agnew quickly won popularity. A national poll named him one of the three most admired men in the country. But just as scandals destroyed President Nixon, they hurt Agnew as well. Accused of taking bribes while serving in Maryland, he was convicted of the lesser charge of failing to pay his income taxes. He resigned as vice president on October 10, 1973. ■

Maryland's judicial branch has four levels of courts. The state has twelve district courts and eight circuit courts that handle local trials. Decisions appealed in these courts are next heard in the court of special appeals. Maryland's highest court is the court of appeals. The governor appoints the seven judges who sit on this court, but the voters must approve their selection during the next general

Inside the Maryland
State House

election after their appointment. Maryland also has orphans' courts, which deal with issues relating to estates. The judges for these courts are elected.

Local Government

Maryland has twenty-three counties and one independent city, Baltimore. Each county has a county seat where county officials

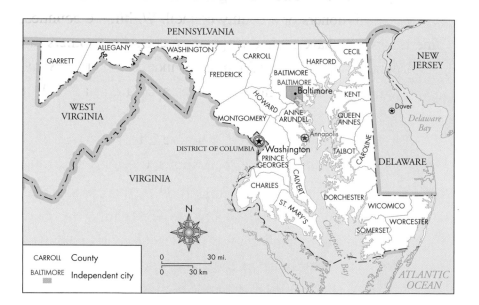

Maryland's counties

From Local Crusader to U.S. Senator

As a political activist, Barbara Mikulski led the fight to save Baltimore neighborhoods from the wrecking ball. In 1968, state and local officials wanted to put a highway through Fells Point, Federal Hill, and West Baltimore. Mikulski and others protested the plans, and community groups convinced politicians to save the neighborhoods. As Mikulski said, "the people got their act together and took control of their own lives."

In 1971, Mikulski won a seat on the Baltimore City Council. Five years later, she turned her sights to a higher national office: the U.S. House of Representatives. In Washington, she continued to fight for the concerns of the working class, people like her neighbors back in East Baltimore. In 1986, Mikulski was elected to the U.S. Senate, making her the first woman to win a statewide election in Maryland. ■

meet to make local laws and handle the county's public affairs. The form of government varies throughout the counties; most have county commissioners or a county council. Within the counties, some towns also have their own governments, while others are unincorporated, meaning they fall directly under county rule. Some of Maryland's largest communities, such as Columbia and Silver Spring, are unincorporated.

Baltimore is sometime called Baltimore City, to distinguish it from a neighboring county with the same name. Baltimore is governed by a mayor and a city council. Maryland is one of only two states with independent cities (not part of a county) in America.

CHAPTER EIGHT

Bay and Fields, Offices and Labs

n its earliest days, Maryland built its wealth on tobacco. By the eighteenth century, other crops helped fuel the colony's economy, as did shipbuilding and trade. The Chesapeake Bay was always an important source of income for some Marylanders, but the oyster and crab industries grew in the nineteenth century, when new technology let the state ship its seafood across the country. Today, Maryland still relies on all the products of its past, but much of the state's economic future is tied to high technology—computers, aerospace, and scientific research of every kind.

Ocean City is a major resort on the Atlantic Coast.

Wealth from the Water

Maryland's great sailing fleets of the past are long gone; by 1980 just thirty skipjacks dredged the Chesapeake Bay for oysters. Maryland's waters, however, still produce more oysters than any other state's, and the total commercial catch of all seafood brings in about $50 million per year. Processing the fish is still an important source of jobs for many Eastern Shore residents.

The Chesapeake Bay also creates jobs as one of Maryland's great tourist attractions. Recreational fishing, boating, and swimming are popular activities in and on the water; many tourists also come to admire the diverse wildlife and the natural beauty that surrounds the bay. Other visitors looking for water fun head to Deep

Opposite: Scientific laboratories play an important role in Maryland's economy.

Creek Lake, in Garrett County, or Ocean City, Maryland's major resort on the Atlantic Ocean. The guests at these destinations—and across the state—stay in hotels, eat at restaurants, buy supplies, and rent equipment, creating more than 77,000 jobs for Maryland's tourism industry. Tourist spending adds about $6 billion to Maryland's economy every year.

From the Mountains and the Land

Maryland's stretch of the Allegheny Mountains once produced more than 5 million tons of coal per year. Today coal production is much lower, but the state still produces a large amount of non-fuel minerals, such as crushed stone, sand, and gravel. Extracting and selling this stone and sand generates more than $300 million every year.

Even more productive are Maryland's farms and nurseries. More than 2 million acres (800,000 ha) of the state's lands are used to grow various crops, though only about 20,000 people work directly on farms. Leading agricultural products are house and garden plants and flowers, corn, and soybeans; the state's orchards also grow a variety of fruit, including peaches and apples. Tobacco is still grown in the southern part of the state.

Thousands of Marylanders process and ship the state's agricultural products for consumption around the world. Maryland also has one of the country's leading spice companies. McCormick and Company, based in Sparks, sells such everyday spices as pepper and basil as well as more exotic flavorings, such as cumin and saffron.

Another leading agricultural activity is raising livestock. Mary-

Opposite: The bounty of Maryland's agriculture

Farming Down to a Science

Can a turkey be too big? Back in the 1940s, some Americans thought so. Too many days of leftovers kept some families from buying the birds except for holidays. That's when scientists at the Beltsville Agricultural Research Center (BARC) stepped in. They bred a new, smaller turkey that was an immediate hit with the country's cooks.

BARC is just one of the many federal research centers that provide jobs for Marylanders and improve life for millions of people. Spread out on 7,000 acres (2,800 ha), the center is the largest agricultural research complex in the world. Its land is divided into pastures, production fields, orchards, and plots where scientists test out new varieties of crops.

In BARC's labs, scientists look for new ways to fight various plant diseases and make tastier fruits, vegetables, and meats. They also look for new uses for old products. For example, BARC researchers recently found a way to turn chicken feathers into paper! The fiber made from the feathers could even be used to replace some plastics. ■

A Tough Man and His Chickens

As a boy in Salisbury, Frank Perdue took care of some fifty chickens, selling their eggs for spending money. His father had already established a small chicken farm, and in 1939 Frank joined the business. Over the years, he turned Perdue Farms into the fourth-largest chicken producer in the nation.

After the company began raising broilers, Perdue turned to science to improve his product. He used computers to regulate how much feed the birds ate and bred new types of meatier, tastier chickens. Perdue also added turkeys and other poultry to the company's product line. In the 1970s, Perdue began appearing in TV ads as spokesperson for the company. The balding man with a nasal voice told viewers that it took a "tough man to make a tender chicken."

In the mid 1990s, Frank Perdue passed day-to-day control of the company to his son James. By then Perdue Farms employed about 18,000 people and annually sold poultry products worth about $2 billion. ■

land farmers raise some cattle and hogs, but they are tops at raising chickens. More than 3 million birds are kept for their eggs, while almost 300 million are raised as "broilers"—the chickens that end up on dinner tables around the world.

Manufacturing

As has happened across the Northeast, many of Maryland's former factories have shrunk their workforce or closed completely. The state, however, still has an important manufacturing industry that employs almost one worker out of every ten. One of the country's

Maryland's natural resources

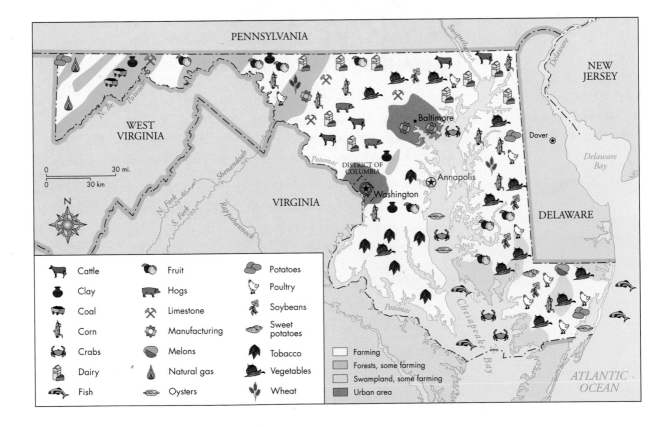

Powerful Tools

In the early 1900s, the United States was already the world's greatest industrialized nation. Much of its wealth came from ingenious people who created improved tools for making other products. Two of these inspired inventors were Duncan Black and Alonzo Decker.

In 1910, Black and Decker took a $1,200 investment and opened a manufacturing company in Baltimore. They made machines for capping bottles and dipping candy into chocolate, but their first important breakthrough was the electric drill—a handheld tool shaped like a large pistol. Black and Decker moved their company to Towson—site of its world headquarters today—and added other products, including the first portable electric screwdriver (1922) and the electric hammer (1936).

Duncan Black died in 1951, and Alonzo Decker died four years later. Today, the company they founded is famous for its portable tools used by both construction professionals and do-it-yourself builders. Black and Decker also introduced the "Dustbuster," a battery-powered hand-held vacuum cleaner that hangs in workshops, kitchens, and playrooms around the globe. ■

major manufacturers of aerospace equipment and sophisticated electronics is Lockheed Martin, based in Bethesda. The company was formed by the mergers of various aviation and electronic companies. The "Martin" in the name refers to Glenn L. Martin, the aviation pioneer who designed the famous clipper plane of the 1930s.

Maryland's manufacturers also make computers, chemical products, and industrial machinery. The state has a large printing industry too, thanks mainly to the various government agencies in and around Washington, D.C.

Aiming to Please

Despite the continued importance of manufacturing and agriculture in Maryland, the state has followed a national trend. It relies on the service sector for most of its jobs. The service sector covers a broad range of businesses and professions, such as office workers, government employees, wholesale and retail sales, doctors,

Bridging the Bay

A healthy economy requires construction—roads, buildings, and houses. One of Maryland's great construction projects of the past, Chesapeake Bay Bridge, helped stimulate tourism and the general economy of the Eastern Shore.

Before the bridge was built, driving to the Eastern Shore from Baltimore or Annapolis meant going halfway around the bay or taking a ferry. State officials first discussed building a bridge in the 1920s, but construction didn't start until 1949. The bridge opened for traffic in 1952, connecting the Western Shore near Annapolis with Kent Island. In 1973, a second span opened next to the first, which in 1967 had been renamed the William Preston Lane Jr. Memorial Bridge, in honor of a former Maryland governor.

The Chesapeake Bay Bridge is one of the world's longest at 93,192 feet (28,405 m), and is supported by more than 4,000 immense steel beams, some of them buried 200 feet (60 m) into the floor of the bay. If drivers feel nervous about crossing long bridges, state employees drive their cars over for them. ■

Charity from a Merchant

Johns Hopkins was a member of Maryland's nineteenth-century service economy—long before the phrase was ever coined. Born in 1795 in Anne Arundel County, Hopkins went to Baltimore as a teenager to work in his uncle's wholesale grocery business. In 1820, Hopkins opened his own business and soon became a successful merchant. He used his profits to open a bank and to build warehouses, which added to Baltimore's reputation as a major commercial city. Hopkins also became a major investor in the B&O Railroad, holding more shares than any other individual stock owner.

Hopkins amassed a huge fortune but lived very frugally. He walked wherever he could, rarely left the city of Baltimore, and once refused to put new carpeting in his house because, he said, he would rather keep the money in the bank earning interest. But in his will, Hopkins showed a more generous side. When he died in 1873, he left $7 million to found Johns Hopkins University and Hospital. ■

lawyers, social workers, and restaurants. Any job that involves helping people is a service job.

Many of Maryland's service employees actually work outside the state, in Washington, D.C. These capital commuters include staff members of the federal government and its many agencies. Other government employees work at the many military installations and federal agencies in Maryland. The U.S. government is the largest employer in Maryland's service sector. Banking and insurance are also part of the service sector, and Baltimore is home to a number of major financial institutions.

A New Kind of Industry

The service economy also includes processing information—banks have to keep track of accounts, teachers and students need to log online for research. Making the computers and software that process this information is a relatively new industry, one that Marylanders have eagerly embraced.

The first computers came to Maryland through the federal government. One was installed at the Aberdeen Proving Ground shortly after World War II and, in the 1960s, the Social Security Administration, based in Baltimore, had one of the largest computers in the country. Today, the computer industry overlaps with many others in Maryland—aerospace, electronics, and government research. New companies continue to spring up around Baltimore and Washington, taking advantage of Maryland's educated workforce and the network of high-tech firms already in place. Interstate 270, in Montgomery County, is sometimes called the "high technology corridor" of the state.

CHAPTER NINE

Life in the Free State

Maryland's population is diverse and continues to grow.

Starting in 1634, the first Europeans to reach Maryland were mostly English. Although the ruling Calvert family was Roman Catholic, other English settlers were Protestant. Africans also came, as servants and then as slaves. Over the centuries, Maryland's population continued to grow and became increasingly diverse. As of 1990, the state had about 4,798,622 people, ranking it nineteenth among the fifty states. The state's population density—the number of people living in each square mile—was 459, fifth in the nation. About 25 percent of Maryland's population is African-American. Asians make up about 3 percent of the state's residents and about 2.6 percent are Hispanic. Only about 20,000 descendants of Maryland's first inhabitants, the Native Americans, remain in the state.

A Place for Immigrants

The early history of Maryland was dominated by the English, and their influence endures in the state's geography. Counties and towns were often named after locations in England or English settlers, such as Talbot, Dorchester, and Somerset. But over the years, immigrants from many lands came to Maryland, just as they spread out all across America. The first significant non-English settlers were the Germans. In 1734, some Germans from Pennsylvania arrived just outside of Frederick. Soon, other Germans came to Baltimore as well. The German community organized a Lutheran

Opposite: Autumn at Hood College

church in the city in 1755, and it became a center of German cultural life.

Religion was usually important for most immigrants; their churches or temples were a link to customs from their homeland. Maryland, with its history of religious tolerance, became the home of many different faiths. Quakers, who were scorned by other Protestants, came to Maryland shortly after the colony was founded. America's first Presbyterian church was started in Snow Hill in 1684. Abingdon was the site of the country's first Methodist college, Cokesbury College, which opened in 1785. Elizabeth Seton, who became America's first native-born Catholic saint, started the country's first parochial school system in Maryland, and the first ordained Jewish rabbi in America came to Baltimore in 1840.

Although Germans and other immigrants settled around the state, Baltimore attracted the greatest diversity of immigrants. Italians, Irish, Poles, Jews, Greeks, Czechs, Russians, and others came to the city in the nineteenth century, usually settling in their own ethnic neighborhoods. During tough economic times, African-Americans from rural parts of the state, such as southern Maryland, came to Baltimore to find jobs. Others came from states south of Maryland. Today, more than half of Baltimore's population is African-American.

Immigrants continue to play an important role in Maryland. Without them, the state's population would be falling. Since 1990, thousands of Marylanders have left the state for other parts of the country. But during that time, a larger number of immigrants settled in Maryland—about 93,000 between 1990 and 1997. Many of these immigrants came from Asia and Latin America.

Where and How People Live

Baltimore has kept its place as Maryland's largest city, with about 650,000 residents as of 1997. Although no longer a major industrial center, Baltimore remains Maryland's chief port and the heart of its business and artistic communities. Many people live and work in the city, while thousands commute daily into Baltimore from the suburbs. The city and its suburbs are at the northern end of a strip of heavily populated communities that stretches to Washington, D.C. Other large communities in this area include Silver Spring, Columbia, Dundalk, and Bethesda. Almost 93 percent of Marylanders live in or near a city.

Most Marylanders live in or near urban areas.

Maryland's smaller cities and suburbs have a mix of businesses, apartments, and neighborhoods of single-family homes. The suburbs in Montgomery and Howard counties are the state's wealthiest. Families in these counties have an average income of more than $64,000 per year, compared to $27,000 for the state as a whole.

Although most Marylanders live in a metropolitan area, the state still has pockets of rural communities, especially in the western and southern parts of the state and along the Eastern Shore. These small towns have all the modern conveniences, but people seem to live at a slower pace than in the cities. One of the more iso-

Population of Maryland's Major Cities (1990)

Baltimore	736,014
Silver Spring	76,046
Columbia	75,883
Dundalk	65,800
Bethesda	62,936

A Shrinking City

At the time of the Civil War, Baltimore was America's third-largest city, with just more than 212,000 residents. It reached its population peak in 1950, when almost 950,000 people called the city home. Since then, Baltimore's population has been gradually declining. In 1990, with 736,014 residents, Baltimore was the thirteenth-largest city in America. Just four years later, the city had lost 32,000 more people and slipped to fourteenth largest in the country. The city expects to lose thousands more by 2000.

Why the steep decline? Baltimore, like many industrial cities of the Northeast, lost many jobs, especially during the economic problems of the mid-1970s and early 1980s. Companies moved their operations to western and southern states or to foreign countries. The people who did have jobs began to move to the suburbs, as improved highways made it easy to commute into the city. People who moved into Baltimore were usually poor, and other Marylanders often thought the city was filled with poverty and crime.

The development of the Inner Harbor as a tourist attraction helped reverse Baltimore's troubled image. But the city will never again have almost a million people living in its many neighborhoods. Maryland officials expect the population decline to continue during the twenty-first century. ■

lated spots in Maryland is Smith Island, just west of Crisfield. About 12 miles (19 km) off the coast, the island was first settled in 1657. Boats take the high school students to school on the mainland. Legend has it that years ago, the island's residents threw oyster shells at any strangers trying to land on their shores. The Smith Islanders enjoyed their isolation from the rest of the state.

Smith Island was settled in 1657.

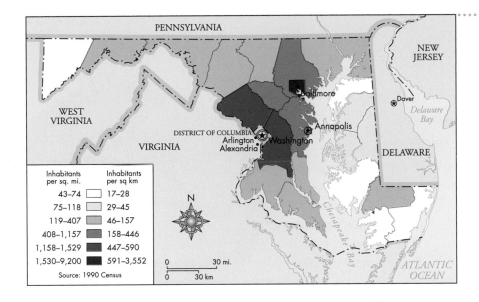

Maryland's population density

Inhabitants per sq. mi. / Inhabitants per sq km
- 43–74 / 17–28
- 75–118 / 29–45
- 119–407 / 46–157
- 408–1,157 / 158–446
- 1,158–1,529 / 447–590
- 1,530–9,200 / 591–3,552

Source: 1990 Census

A Maryland Dining Tradition

Maryland is famous for its seafood, especially crabs. "There is a saying in Baltimore," H. L. Mencken wrote, "that crabs may be prepared in fifty ways and that all of them are good." Crabs can come cooked in a rich casserole or steamed in the shell, their sweet flesh plucked out by patient diners. Crab cakes are also a treat, a delicious mixture of crabmeat, bread crumbs, eggs, and spices. But when true fans of shellfish think of Maryland, they think of eating freshly caught blue crabs—shell and all.

Most people know these crustaceans as soft-shelled crabs, though they're often simply called soft crabs in Maryland. They can be grilled, deep-fried, sautéed in butter, or buried under a spicy sauce. The soft crab is a blue crab that has actually shed its shell, also called a carapace. The crabs are caught and served before the new carapace has a chance to harden, though it still usually has a little crunch. Some folks are squeamish about eating the whole crab, claws and all, but to many people, soft-shelled crabs are a Maryland delicacy. ■

Crab Cakes

Ingredients:

1 lb. Maryland crab meat, backfin or special, with all cartilage removed

1/2 cup white bread crumbs

1 large egg, beaten

1/4 cup mayonnaise

2 teaspoons Worcestershire sauce

1 teaspoon mustard

1 teaspoon Old Bay seasoning

salt and pepper to taste

vegetable oil for frying

lemon wedges

Directions:

Mix the bread crumbs, egg, mayonnaise, Worcestershire sauce, mustard, Old Bay seasoning, and salt and pepper in a large bowl. Add crab meat and mix well, but gently. Form six crab cakes with your hands.

Ask your mom or dad to deep-fry the cakes until they are golden brown on each side. You can also sauté the cakes (5 minutes each side) or broil them (5–7 minutes or until golden brown).

Serve with lemon wedges.

Serves 3.

English with a Twist

The isolation of people on Smith Island has given them a distinct accent. Some people can hear a trace of a British accent in the English spoken on the island. The residents are descendants of some of Maryland's earliest English settlers.

In other parts of the state, Marylanders speak with what sounds like an accent to a stranger—but of course, to the Marylanders, it's

Eastern Shore Speak

For many years, the residents of the Eastern Shore felt like a separate part of Maryland. On several occasions they even tried to split off and form their own state. In their remote location across Chesapeake Bay, the people on the Eastern Shore developed their own unique expressions. Here's a sample of Eastern Shore dialect.

When Eastern Shore People Say:	They Mean:
A come here	A person not born on the Eastern Shore
A woman has "gone to Canaan"	She's pregnant
A crab is a Jimmy	It's a male crab
A crab is a Sooky (or Sook)	It's a female crab
Big day	A family dinner
Bay Sider	Someone who lives west of the railroad tracks
Sea Sider	Someone who lives east of the railroad tracks
Little nicks	Small clams
Jag	A large catch of oysters
Protracted meeting	A church revival
Back house	An outhouse
Blue hen's chicken	A wild and unruly young person

the outsider who speaks with an accent! Baltimoreans are known for their accent, which makes the name of their city sound like "Bawlamer." And on the Eastern Shore, the locals have created their own slang words for a number of expressions.

Love of Learning

The English settlers of Maryland believed in the power of education, and today the state continues its long tradition of academic excellence. Its first college was Washington College, in Chestertown. Opened in 1782, Washington is the tenth-oldest college in the

The dome of the
medical school at
Johns Hopkins
University

country. The school was named for General George Washington, who helped sell lottery tickets to fund the college. In 1807, Maryland state officials founded the University of Maryland at Baltimore, the state's largest university. More than 30,000 students attend the campus at College Park, and thousands more go to the university's branches in Baltimore, Baltimore County, and Princess Anne, on the Eastern Shore.

Baltimore is also the home of Johns Hopkins University, with its famous medical school. Johns Hopkins receives more government funding for research than any other university in the country. Other Baltimore colleges and universities include Towson University and Loyola College, a Jesuit school. Maryland is the home of America's oldest Catholic college, Mount Saint Mary's. Located in Emmitsburg, the school opened in 1808. The following year, St. Joseph's College for Women opened nearby.

Other notable colleges and universities in Maryland include the U.S. Naval Academy in Annapolis, Hood College in Frederick, Western Maryland College in Westminster, Salisbury State University in Salisbury, and St. Mary's College of Maryland in St. Mary's City.

For elementary and high school students, Maryland has twenty-four districts that handle public education—one for each county and Baltimore City. About 52,800 teachers instruct more than 800,000 children. Other students attend private schools, such as the Landon School, a well-known prep school in Bethesda, or schools run by churches. Students in Baltimore can add to their learning at the Enoch Pratt Free Library. Its twenty-eight branches have more than 2.7 million books, magazines, and other items.

Classic College

St. John's College gives its students a typical liberal arts education, including courses in English, history, science, and the arts. But the students learn these subjects in an unusual way. Instead of poring over modern textbooks, the young scholars read classics by ancient Greek and Roman authors and other works judged to be the most important books ever written.

St. John's officially opened in 1784, taking over the grounds and the teachers of King William's School, an Annapolis grammar school founded in 1696. The idea to use the classics to teach college students came in 1937. The original list of 100 books has been expanded and changed over time, but students still focus on the classics.

The campus of St. John's has a famous landmark—the last surviving Liberty Tree. Before the Revolutionary War, patriots known as the Sons of Liberty met in towns across the colonies to discuss independence. The Sons usually gathered around trees nicknamed "Liberty trees." The Annapolis Liberty Tree is a tulip poplar at least 400 years old. ■

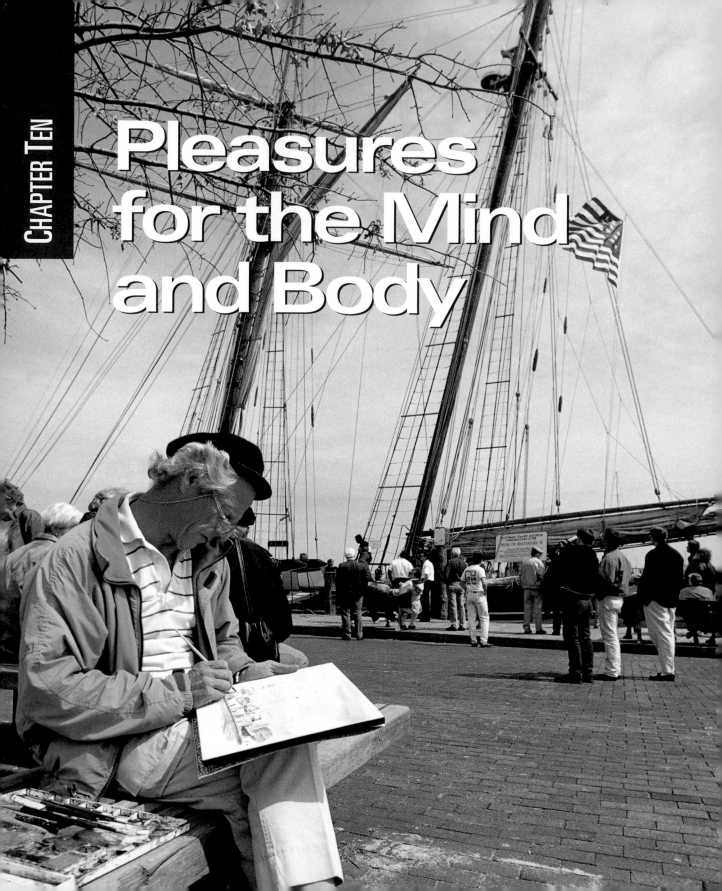

CHAPTER TEN

Pleasures for the Mind and Body

Wherever they live and whatever they do, Marylanders enjoy a variety of creative pursuits and leisure activities. The state has produced a number of talented writers, artists, and musicians who beautifully capture the details of human life and emotions—from the comic to the tragic. Their works have enlightened not only other Marylanders, but also United States citizens, and people around the world.

Maryland is also famous for a number of world-class athletes. Their skills and competitive drive entertain the state's sports fans, who also take time to pursue their own favorite physical activities. The variety of sports and arts found in Maryland reflect its claim to be "America in miniature."

Raising Thoroughbred horses is big business in Maryland.

A Talent for Words

The first Maryland authors were the letter-writers and journal-keepers of the seventeenth century. Father Andrew White's account of the Calvert settlement, *A Briefe Relation of the Voyage unto Maryland,* was followed by similar writings by other settlers. In 1666, an indentured servant named George Alsop wrote a lengthy description of Maryland called *A Character of the Province of Maryland.* The work pleased Lord Baltimore because Alsop wrote so favorably of the colony. In one poem in his work, Alsop called Maryland "the only emblem of tranquillity."

Opposite: Sketching at Baltimore's harbor

Another early poet who visited Maryland was not so pleased with life in the colony. In 1708, a tobacco merchant named Ebenezer Cooke wrote *The Sot-Weed Factor* (sot-weed was another name for tobacco). Cooke wrote about the diseases and harsh life that awaited settlers in Maryland. He called Annapolis "A City Situated on a Plain/Where scarce a house will keep out the Rain."

In the early days of the United States, a Maryland minister named Mason Locke Weems won fame for his writing. Weems wrote a glowing biography of George Washington. The work is best remembered today as the source of the legend that Washington once chopped down a cherry tree, then confessed to his naughty act.

Nineteenth- and Twentieth-Century Writers

Maryland's best-known author of the nineteenth century was Edgar Allan Poe. His great reputation reached its peak after his death, but another Maryland writer was famous during his own lifetime. The former slave and abolitionist Frederick Douglass wrote his autobiography in 1845, *Narrative of the Life of Frederick Douglass, an American Slave*. Twice during his life he revised the work. Another former Maryland slave who wrote about his experiences was Josiah Henson. His book, *Truth Stranger Than Fiction*, inspired Harriet Beecher Stowe to write her famous antislavery novel *Uncle Tom's Cabin*.

In the twentieth century, Maryland has been associated with a number of well-known writers. Some were born in the state; oth-

Master of Mystery and Horror

"Once upon a midnight dreary, while I pondered, weak and weary." So begins Allan Poe's most famous poem, "The Raven." The black bird crushes the poet's dreams of his true love Lenore by endlessly repeating "Nevermore."

Poe was a master at creating eerie settings and scary scenes. In "The Tell-Tale Heart," a murderer confesses his crime as he thinks he hears the beating heart of his victim. A house sinks into the earth after the death of its residents in "The Fall of the House of Usher." Poe is also considered the inventor of the detective story, with his tale "The Murders in the Rue Morgue."

Born in Boston in 1809, Poe first came to Baltimore in 1831. He lived with his aunt, staying until 1835. Poe had already written three volumes of poetry, but his career took off in Baltimore. He won a writing contest with the short story "The Ms. Found in a Bottle" and became editor of a literary magazine. After leaving Baltimore to work elsewhere, Poe returned in 1849. Always a somewhat sad and troubled man, Poe died after being found in the street near a tavern. A heart attack, possibly aided by alcohol, led to his death. Poe is buried in Baltimore's Westminster Churchyard. ■

ers lived there for a time, and some spent their last days there. Perhaps the writer most closely associated with Maryland—specifically Baltimore—is H. L. Mencken. A newspaper reporter and columnist for many years, Mencken wrote witty attacks on American values and America's sometimes silly people. "The men [Americans] detest most violently," he wrote in 1918, "are those that try to tell them the truth."

Another humorous writer who lived in Baltimore was the poet Ogden Nash. He published twenty volumes of "light" verse and

Anne Tyler set many novels in Baltimore.

Charles Willson Peale was known for his portraits of George Washington, Thomas Jefferson, Benjamin Franklin, and others.

also wrote books for children. A more serious writer associated with Baltimore is novelist F. Scott Fitzgerald. He lived in the city for three years, and he and his wife Zelda are buried in Rockville.

Famous writers born in Maryland include Dashiell Hammett, Tom Clancy, and John Barth. Hammett, born in St. Mary's County, created the detective Sam Spade, hero of the novel and film *The Maltese Falcon*. Baltimore native Clancy published his first novel, *The Hunt for Red October*, in 1984. His books are modern thrillers, blending high-technology gadgets with world politics. In 1997, Clancy signed a $100-million contract, making him the highest-paid author in history. Unlike these two popular authors, Barth is known for his serious literature, such as *Giles Goat-Boy* and *Lost in the Funhouse*. Born in Cambridge, Barth sometimes uses Eastern Shore locales in his work. Another respected novelist with ties to Maryland is Anne Tyler. She lived in Baltimore and set many of her books in the city. In 1989, she won the Pulitzer Prize for fiction for *Breathing Lessons*.

Art for the Eyes

Starting in the 18th century, Maryland was the home of many talented visual artists. Justus Engelhart Kuhn, born in Germany, worked in Annapolis from 1708 to 1717. He was one of the first artists in America to depict a slave in a formal painting. In the latter part of the century, Maryland native Charles Willson Peale was one of the country's most famous painters. Born in Chestertown, Peale painted a number of portraits of George Washington and his other subjects included Thomas Jefferson. Peale named at least five of his sons after famous European artists. Two of them,

A Cherished Church

A cathedral is not just any church—its size and splendor are meant to awe the people who worship in it. In 1821, the U.S.'s first Roman Catholic cathedral opened in Baltimore, and it still impresses visitors with its dome, mighty columns, and bells that ring out three times a day.

The cathedral is officially called the Basilica of the Assumption of the Blessed Virgin Mary. Bishop John Carroll, America's first Roman Catholic bishop, hired Benjamin Latrobe to design the building (Latrobe also designed the U.S. Capitol in Washington, D.C.). The architect borrowed styles from the ancient Greeks and Romans for this massive structure and used granite from nearby Ellicott City to build it. Architectural historians consider Latrobe's design one of the most notable American buildings of the early nineteenth century.

Inside, the cathedral has an organ dating back to 1821, an altar donated by French citizens and paintings that were gifts from France's King Louis XVIII. Under the cathedral is a crypt where Bishop Carroll and other Baltimore bishops are buried. ■

Rembrandt and Raphaelle, were also successful artists, and Rembrandt opened one of the first public art museums in America. This Baltimore institution was known as the Peale Museum.

Baltimore's fame as the "Monumental City" rests on a number of well-known monuments. One, the Washington Monument, was one of the first major monuments in America erected to honor the nation's first president. The monument was designed by architect Robert Mills, who moved to Baltimore in 1815. He also designed the Washington Monument in the nation's capital. Maximilian Godefroy, a French-born architect, came to the city in 1805 and later designed the Battle Monument, along with a number of churches and Baltimore's Merchant's Exchange Building.

Maryland is also known for a unique folk art—wooden decoys.

Museum of Modern Masters

Maryland's art lovers can pursue their passion at one of America's finest museums, the Baltimore Museum of Art (BMA). Founded in 1929, the museum now has more than 85,000 objects in its collection, and a library with 50,000 books and magazines. Outside, patrons can stroll through almost 3 acres (1.2 ha) of sculpture.

The BMA has art from around the world and dating back to the sixteenth century and before, but it's best known for its modern art. The museum's Cone Collection was once the private collection of two Baltimore sisters, Claribel and Etta Cone. In the early twentieth century, they often traveled to Paris to buy works by such modern masters as Pablo Picasso, Paul Cezanne, and Vincent Van Gogh. The Cones also bought 500 pieces by the French artist Henri Matisse—the world's largest collection of his work.

The museum's West Wing features sixteen galleries dedicated to art and sculpture created after 1945. One of the highlights of this collection is more than a dozen pieces by the American pop artist Andy Warhol. The BMA has one of the world's largest public displays of his work. ■

Hunters along the Chesapeake Bay rely on these decoys to attract waterfowl, and carving and painting them is a great skill. The Havre de Grace Decoy Museum honors the state's many talented decoy carvers.

Stagecraft

The performing arts include music, theater, opera, and dance. Baltimore is Maryland's capital for these dynamic art forms. The Meyerhoff Symphony Hall, the home of the Baltimore Symphony Orchestra and Chorus, is famous for its brilliant acoustics. The city's opera company performs at the Lyric Opera House. Concerts

The Baltimore Symphony Orchestra makes its home in Meyerhoff Symphony Hall.

are also held at the Peabody Conservatory, the Baltimore Arena, and an outdoor arena at the Inner Harbor. The city has at least half a dozen theaters and acting companies. Center Stage is considered the finest in Maryland. The Morris A. Mechanic Theater attracts touring Broadway shows, and the Arena Players are a respected African-American theater company.

Singer Billie Holiday was born in Baltimore.

The performing arts are also represented in other cities across Maryland. Annapolis is home of the Maryland Hall for the Creative Arts, which features classical music, opera, and ballet. Frederick has the Weinberg Center for the Arts, where theater, music, and dance are performed. The Cumberland Theater is that city's performing arts center.

Maryland's creative citizens have included a number of world-famous jazz musicians. Chick Webb, a jazz band leader of the 1930s and 1940s, was born in Baltimore. So was one of the greatest jazz singers of all time, Billie "Lady Day" Holiday. Another Baltimore native, Larry Adler, is a famous jazz harmonica player.

Wild about Eubie

In the 1920s, many white Americans discovered jazz for the first time. The man who helped introduce them to this toe-tapping music was James Hubert "Eubie" Blake. The son of former slaves, Blake was born in Baltimore in 1883. He first learned about music by playing gospel songs on his family's organ, then took lessons in classical music. But ragtime, the popular African-American music of the day, became his great love. "It just swung," he said, and "made me feel good."

Blake used his skills to make others feel good, too. In 1921, he composed the music for a Broadway show called *Shuffle Along*. The songs included "Love Will Find a Way" and "I'm Just Wild About Harry." The show was a hit, as white listeners embraced ragtime. Later, in 1948, President Harry Truman used "Harry" as his theme song during the 1948 presidential campaign. Blake continued to write and perform music until his death in 1983. Today, music fans can learn more about ragtime and Blake's life at Baltimore's Eubie Blake National Museum and Cultural Center. ■

On the Field

Baseball is called America's national pastime, and it's a favorite sport of Marylanders as well. Since the late nineteenth century, Baltimore has been the home of various teams known as the Orioles; the current Orioles joined the major leagues in 1954. In the early part of the twentieth century, the Baltimore teams perfected a style of baseball that relied on speed and cunning. The players invented the "Baltimore chop"—a ball deliberately hit down into the ground so that it would bounce high enough to let the batter reach first base. In the 1960s and 1970s, the Orioles had some of the best teams in baseball, featuring such future Hall of Famers as Brooks and Frank Robinson, Jim Palmer, and manager Earl Weaver.

Baseball's Iron Man

Injuries are a part of any sport, making it rare for a player to complete a season without missing a game. Cal Ripken Jr., however, made a habit of playing through pain. On September 6, 1995, the Baltimore Orioles infielder set a major league record when he played in his 2,131st consecutive game, breaking the old record set by Lou Gehrig of the New York Yankees. Although Ripken did not play every inning of every game during his record-setting streak, at one point he did play more than 8,000 consecutive innings. On September 20, 1998, Cal Ripken Jr. ended his consecutive-games streak at 2,632.

Ripken was born in Havre de Grace. As a teen, he used to take batting practice at the Orioles' old park—Memorial Stadium—when his father was a coach for the team. Cal Jr. joined the Orioles late in the team's 1981 season and started his consecutive-game streak on May 30, 1982. He hit 28 home runs that year, showed great fielding ability, and was named the American League Rookie of the Year. The following year, Ripken beat the "sophomore jinx" with a .318 batting average, 27 home runs, and 102 runs batted in. That performance earned him the league's Most Valuable Player award. He won that honor again in 1991. His skills and dedication guarantee Ripken a spot in Baseball's Hall of Fame. ■

In football, Maryland fans just recently reacquired their own National Football League team. The Baltimore Colts left Maryland in 1984 to play in Indianapolis. Before then, the Colts had a history of great players, including quarterback Johnny Unitas and running back Lenny Moore. In 1971, the Colts beat the Dallas Cowboys to win Super Bowl V. Football returned to Baltimore in 1996, when the Cleveland Browns came to the city and became the Ravens. A

Baseball at Camden Yards

Although Babe Ruth never played at Oriole Park, he is part of the history of the stadium. Ruth, one of baseball's greatest sluggers during the 1920s and 1930s, was born in Baltimore. Oriole Park at Camden Yards sits on the site where Ruth's father once owned a saloon, and the young Babe often played in the neighborhood streets.

Oriole Park opened in 1992, and it quickly became a favorite tourist spot for baseball fans across America, even when the Orioles weren't in town. Able to hold 48,000 spectators, the park has the feel of an old-fashioned stadium, with its natural grass and open stands. Unlike some modern parks, Oriole Park was built exclusively for baseball.

Behind the stadium's right and centerfield seats is the B&O Railroad Warehouse, now used as an office building, and Camden Station. The railway station opened in 1856, and for twenty years the only railroad from Washington, D.C., to the North ran through it. Still a train depot, Camden Station is now also the home of the Babe Ruth Baseball Center, a tribute to baseball in Baltimore. ■

new stadium opened in 1998, next to the widely praised baseball stadium, Oriole Park at Camden Yards.

In amateur sports, many Marylanders follow the successful football and basketball programs at the University of Maryland. Graduates include pro football stars Randy White and Boomer Esiason. Navy also attracts fans to its football and basketball games in Annapolis. NFL quarterback Roger Staubach and NBA center David Robinson were midshipmen at the Naval Academy.

Raising and racing horses has a long tradition in Maryland. Races were common in the eighteenth century, and some wealthy Marylanders also used their horses to hunt foxes. The Maryland Hunt Cup was first run in 1894. It is considered by many to be the toughest timber race in the world, covering a 4-mile (6.4-km)

Pimlico hosts the Preakness Triple Crown race each year.

Going for the Goal

Lacrosse is the oldest team sport in North America. In the seventeenth century, French and English colonists in Canada saw Native Americans playing the game, using sticks to knock a ball into a goal. The rules for modern lacrosse were first developed around 1867. The name of the game comes from the French word *crosier*—a long stick with a curved end often carried by religious figures. A lacrosse stick resembles a crosier.

A men's lacrosse team has ten players, while a women's team has twelve. Each player is equipped with a stick that has a netted basket at the end. Players try to shoot a rubber ball into a goal, while a goalie and the other defenders try to stop the shots. Helmets and pads help protect the players from injury when they're hit by the ball or an opponent's stick.

In college lacrosse, teams from Johns Hopkins University and the University of Maryland are among the best in the country. The two schools have a fierce rivalry dating back to 1895. ■

course of twenty-two timber fences. Today, one of America's greatest horse racing events, the Preakness, is held each year at Baltimore's Pimlico Race Track. First held in 1873, the Preakness is one of three "Triple Crown" racing events.

Two amateur sports are popular throughout Maryland: the state sport of jousting and lacrosse. The first jousting tournaments were held in the state in 1842. Lacrosse, a fast-paced sport played with sticks and a ball, has its Hall of Fame at Johns Hopkins University.

Timeline

United States History

1607 The first permanent British settlement is established in North America at Jamestown.

1620 Pilgrims found Plymouth Colony, the second permanent British settlement.

1776 America declares its independence from England.

1783 Treaty of Paris officially ends the Revolutionary War in America.

1787 U.S. Constitution is written.

1803 Louisiana Purchase almost doubles the size of the United States.

1812–15 U.S. and Britain fight the War of 1812.

Maryland State History

1524 Giovanni da Verrazano sails past Chesapeake Bay, the first European to see it.

1608 Chesapeake Bay is mapped by John Smith.

1634 Calvert settlers reach Chesapeake Bay in March. Leonard Calvert buys land from the Yaocamaco Indians and founds Maryland's first capital.

1649 The Religious Toleration Act is passed, making religious freedom official in Maryland.

1664 Slavery becomes legal in Maryland.

1692 English rulers make the Church of England Maryland's church. Two years later, they move the capital to Annapolis.

1729 Baltimore Town is founded on the Patapsco River.

1788 Maryland approves the Constitution on April 28 and becomes the seventh state in the Union.

1814 British troops invade Baltimore on September 12, then begin shelling Fort McHenry by water. American troops defend the fort and force the British to withdraw.

United States History

Maryland State History

Fast Facts

Black-eyed Susan

The Wye Oak

Statehood date	April 28, 1788, the 7th state
Origin of state name	For Queen Henrietta Maria, wife of Charles I of England
State capital	Annapolis
State nicknames	Old Line State, Free State, Pine Tree State, Lumber State
State motto	*Fatti Maschii, Parole Femine* (Manly deeds, womanly words)
State bird	Baltimore oriole
State flower	Black-eyed Susan
State fish	Striped bass or rockfish
State dog	Chesapeake Bay retriever
State insect	Baltimore checkerspot butterfly
State song	"Maryland, My Maryland"
State tree	White oak
State fair	Timonium (late August-early September)
Total area; rank	12,297 sq. mi. (31,850 sq km); 42nd
Land; rank	9,775 sq. mi. (25,317 sq km); 42nd
Water; rank	2,522 sq. mi. (6,532 sq km); 16th
***Inland water;* rank**	680 sq. mi. (1,761 sq km); 31st

Harborplace

Chesapeake Bay

Coastal water; **rank**	1,842sq. mi. (4,770 sq km); 4th
Geographic center	Prince Georges, 4.5 miles (7.2 km) north west of Davidsonville
Latitude and longitude	Maryland is located approximately between 37° 53′ and 39° 43′ N and 75° 04′ and 79° 29′ W
Highest point	Backbone Mountain, 3,360 feet (1,025 m)
Lowest point	Sea level along the coastline
Largest city	Baltimore
Number of counties	23
Population; rank	4,798,622 (1990 census); 19th
Density	459 persons per sq. mi. (177 per sq km)
Population distribution	81% urban, 19% rural

Ethnic distribution		
(does not equal 100%)	White	70.98%
	Hispanic	2.62%
	Native American	0.27%
	African-American	24.89%
	Asian and Pacific Islanders	2.92%
	Other	0.94%

Record high temperature	109°F (43°C) in Allegany County on July 3, 1898, and at Cumberland and Frederick on July 10, 1936
Record low temperature	−40°F (−40°C) at Oakland on January 13, 1912
Average July temperature	75°F (24°C)

Average January temperature	33°F (1°C)
Average annual precipitation	43 inches (109 cm)

South Mountain

Natural Areas and Historic Sites

National Historic Parks

Harper's Ferry National Historic Park honors many events in the nation's history, including John Brown's attack on slavery and the arrival of the first American railroad. It covers more than 2,300 acres (932 ha) in Maryland and two other states.

The Chesapeake and Ohio Canal National Historic Park follows the route of the Potomac River, from Cumberland, Maryland, to Washington, D.C. Visitors there can ride down the canal in mule-drawn canal boats.

National Scenic Trails

The Appalachian National Scenic Trail runs through Maryland, from Maine to Georgia. It is excellent for bird-watching and hiking, and visitors can enjoy the gorgeous views.

The Potomac Heritage National Scenic Trail became part of the National Scenic Trail System in 1983. It is currently being groomed to outline features of the Potomac River Basin.

National Battlefields

Antietam National Battlefield marks the site where General Robert E. Lee waged his first invasion against the North. Every September 17, Antietam has a ceremony to remember the Battle of Antietam.

Monocacy National Battlefield is the site of the "Battle that Saved Washington," near Frederick. Visitors can see Gambrill's Mill, which served as a hospital during the American Civil War, and Best Farm,

The Battle of Antietam

which protected both the Union and Confederate soldiers from one another.

National Seashore

At *Assateague Island National Seashore*, clamming, crabbing, surf-fishing, and swimming can all be enjoyed by sightseers. Also breathtaking are the wild horses that run along the beaches as well as the 300 species of birds.

National Historic Sites

Clara Barton National Historic Site includes the house of the famous nurse of the American Civil War. Barton's house served as Red Cross headquarters and was designed by Barton herself.

At the *Hampton National Historic Site,* people can tour the spectacular Georgian mansion and gardens. The mansion was finished in 1790 and was the largest house in the United States.

Thomas Stone National Historic Site contains Haberdventure—the home of the Maryland statesman and signer of the Declaration of Independence. In the mid-1990s, his house was being restored to its original eighteenth-century condition.

National Monument

At *Fort McHenry*, visitors can see the restored barracks, flagpole, and military memorabilia. It marks the site of the birthplace of the U.S. national anthem.

National Parkway

George Washington Memorial Parkway connects Mount Vernon to the Great Falls of the Potomac River.

State Forests and Parks

Maryland has more than forty state parks and forests, located on 280,000 acres (113,400 ha) of the state's land. From any point in the state, tourists can drive to a park or forest in forty minutes or less.

Diamondback terrapin

A Maryland forest

Sports Teams

NCAA Teams (Division 1)

Coppin State College Eagles

Loyola College Greyhounds

Morgan State University Bears

Mount St. Mary's College Mountaineers

Towson State University Tigers

U.S. Naval Academy Midshipmen

University of Maryland–Baltimore County Retrievers

University of Maryland–College Park Terrapins

University of Maryland–Eastern Shore Hawks

Major League Baseball

Baltimore Orioles

National Basketball Association

Washington Wizards

National Football League

Baltimore Ravens

National Hockey League

Washington Capitals

Lacrosse

Cultural Institutions

Libraries

Johns Hopkins University Library system consists of numerous specialized libraries, including Welch Medical Library, which serves one of the most prestigious medical schools in the world. Welch has more than 380,000 volumes of texts and a medical archive.

Enoch Pratt Free Library, Baltimore's public library, hosts many special events, such as readings and workshops. It also provides computer classes at its Pratt Center for Technical Training and sponsors the Exploration Center at the children's museum.

The *Maryland Historical Society* contains prints, photographs, and manuscript collections on all aspects of the state's history. It also conducts genealogy workshops so that people can trace their family's ancestry within Maryland.

Museums

The largest art museum in Maryland is the *Baltimore Museum of Art*. Its permanent collection has more than 90,000 works of art.

The *Baltimore Streetcar Museum* displays photos and other memorabilia from Baltimore's streetcar history.

At the Baltimore Museum of Art

The *Chesapeake Bay Maritime Museum* (St. Michael's) sits on 18 acres (7.3 ha) and is housed in nine exhibit buildings. Visitors can tour the restored Hooper Strait lighthouse, originally built in 1879.

The *National Museum of Civil War Medicine* (Annapolis) contains numerous manuscripts, documents, and books about medicine and medical practices used during the American Civil War.

The *U.S. Naval Academy Museum* (Annapolis) honors the soldiers who serve in the U.S. Navy and strives to preserve the theories and actions of sea power.

Performing Arts

Maryland has one opera company, one symphony orchestra, and one professional theater company.

Universities and Colleges

In the mid-1990s, Maryland had thirty-three public and twenty-four private institutions of higher learning.

St. John's College

Annual Events

January–March

Winterfest in McHenry (March)

Maryland Days in St. Mary's City (weekend closest to March 25)

April–June

Maryland Hunt Cup in Baltimore (April)

Ward World Championship Wildfowl Carving Competition in Ocean City (April)

Preakness Celebration in Baltimore (May)

Commissioning Week at the U.S. Naval Academy in Annapolis (May)

Bay County Music Festival in Centreville (June)

Tangier Sound Country Music Festival in Crisfield (June)

July–September

American Indian Inter-Tribal Cultural Powwow in McHenry (July)

Artscape in Baltimore (July)

Rocky Gap Music Festival in Cumberland (August)

Maryland State Fair at Timonium (late August)

National Hard Crab Derby in Crisfield (Labor Day weekend)

Defender's Day Celebration in Baltimore (September)

October–December

Autumn Glory Festival in Garrett County (October)

Fair Hill International three-day Event and Carriage-Driving Championships in Elkton (October)

Olde Princess Anne Days in Somerset County (October)

Chesapeake Appreciation Day Festival near Annapolis (late October)

Waterfowl Festival in Easton (November)

Candlelight tour of Havre de Grace (early December)

Jousting

Thurgood Marshall

Famous People

Benjamin Banneker (1731–1806)	Mathematician
Charles Carroll (1737–1832)	Revolutionary leader and public official
Samuel Chase (1741–1811)	U.S. Supreme Court justice
John Dickinson (1732–1808)	Colonial figure and public official
Frederick Douglass (1818?–1895)	Civil rights leader
John Hanson (1721–1783)	President under the Articles of Confederation
Billie Holiday (1915–1959)	Singer
Francis Scott Key (1779–1843)	Lawyer and poet
Thurgood Marshall (1908–1993)	U.S. Supreme Court justice
Henry Louis Mencken (1880–1956)	Journalist, editor, and critic
Charles Willson Peale (1741–1827)	Artist and naturalist
Edgar Allan Poe (1809–1849)	Author
James Rumsey (1743–1792)	Inventor
George Herman (Babe) Ruth (1895–1948)	Baseball player
Upton Beall Sinclair (1878–1968)	Author and social reformer
Roger Brooke Taney (1777–1864)	U.S. chief justice
Harriet Tubman (1820–1913)	Abolitionist
Leon Uris (1924–)	Author
Mason Locke (Parson) Weems (1759–1825)	Author

To Find Out More

History

- Block, Victor, and Fyllis Hockman. *The Pelican Guide to Maryland*. 2nd ed. Gretna, La.: Pelican Publishing, 1995.

- Fradin, Dennis Brindell. *Maryland*. Danbury, Conn.: Children's Press, 1994.

- Fradin, Dennis Brindell. *The Maryland Colony*. Chicago: Childrens Press, 1990.

- Johnston, Joyce. *Maryland*. Minneapolis: Lerner Publications Company, 1992.

- Marck, John T. *Maryland: The Seventh State*. 4th ed. Glen Arms, Md.: Creative Impressions, 1998.

- St. George, Judith. *Mason and Dixon's Line of Fire*. New York: G. P. Putnam's Sons, 1991.

- Thompson, Kathleen. *Maryland*. Austin, Tex.: Raintree/Steck Vaughn, 1996.

Fiction

- Curtis, Alice Turner. *A Little Maid of Maryland* (Little Maid Historical Series). Illus. by Nat Little. Bedford, Mass.: Applewood Books, 1996.

Biographies

- Burns, Bree. *Harriet Tubman*. Broomall, Penn: Chelsea House Publishers, 1994.

- Douglass, Frederick. *Escape from Slavery: The Boyhood of Frederick Douglass in His Own Words*. Illus. by Michael McCurdy. New York: Knopf, 1994.

- Goldberg, Jake. *Rachel Carson*. Broomall, Penn.: Chelsea House Publishers, 1991.

- Levert, Suzanne. *Edgar Allan Poe*. Broomall, Penn.: Chelsea House Publishers, 1992.

- Sanford, William R. *Babe Ruth*. New York: Crestwood House, 1992.

Websites

- **Sailor**
  http://www.sailor.lib.md.us
  Maryland's online public information network, providing links to library, schools, and other Internet sites.

- **Maryland Electronic Capital**
  http://www.mec.state.md.us
  Gives information on government agencies and state offices

- **Maryland Office of Tourism Development**
  http://www.mdisfun.org
  Connects users to various tourist sites in the state, such as outdoor recreation and shopping areas

- **Maryland Historical Society**
  http://www.mdhs.org/mdhs. html
  For information about the history of Maryland's people and culture

Addresses

- **State House**
  Annapolis, MD 21401
  To contact the governor, senators, or members of the House of Representatives

- **State Library Resource Center/Central Library**
  Enoch Pratt Free Library
  400 Cathedral Street
  Baltimore, MD 21201
  The main library in Maryland's public library system. Provides information about other libraries and resources in the state.

- **Maryland Historical Society**
  201 W. Monument Street
  Baltimore, MD 21201
  To find information on the state's history

- **Maryland Office of Travel and Tourism**
  217 E. Redwood Street
  9th Floor
  Baltimore, MD 21202
  Provides information on recreation in the state

Index

Page numbers in *italics* indicate illustrations.

Meet the Author

Before writing this book, I had visited Maryland but I didn't really know its fascinating history or appreciate its great beauty. Another trip—all too short—took me all over the state, where I had the chance to visit historical sites, talk to the natives, and feel the pride Marylanders take in their state.

My stops included museums not mentioned in this book but still useful for my research, including the B&O Railroad Museum and the Museum of Industry in Baltimore; the Frederick County Historical Society Museum; and the Banneker-Douglass Museum in Annapolis. I met and talked with the people who work at these museums, as well as with typical Marylanders from all walks of life. They all helped me understand Maryland's charms.

Back at home, I dug into books, made phone calls, and searched the Internet, looking for even more information. Some of the sources I used are listed in "To Find Out More." One book not

listed there was especially helpful in my research: *Maryland: A Middle Temperament, 1634–1980*, by Robert Brugger. It's filled with details on the history of the state.

Maryland is the third book I've written for Children's Press. My first two, *England* and *Argentina*, are part of the True Books series. My other nonfiction works include a biography of Secretary of State Madeleine Albright and books on immigration, natural and man-made disasters, and sports. I've also written fiction for children, including adaptations of the classic novels *Don Quixote*, *Frankenstein*, and *The Red Badge of Courage*. I graduated from the University of Connecticut with a BA in History and studied playwriting for one year at Boston's Emerson College. I currently live in Hartford, Connecticut.

Photo Credits